HALLUCINOGENS: CROSS-CULTURAL PERSPECTIVES

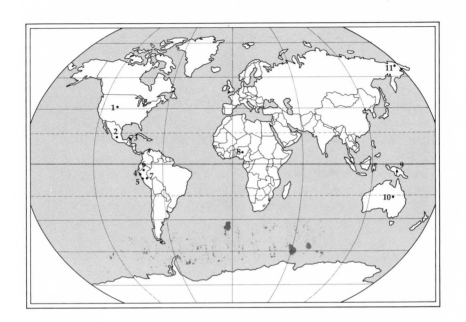

HALLUCINOGENS:

Cross~Cultural Perspectives

Marlene Dobkin de Rios

University of New Mexico Press
Albuquerque

Library of Congress Cataloging in Publication Data

De Rios, Marlene Dobkin.
  Hallucinogens, cross-cultural perspectives.

  Bibliography: p.
  Includes index.
  1. Hallucinogenic plants—Cross-cultural studies. 2. Hallucinogenic
drugs and religious experience—Cross-cultural studies. I. Title.
GN472.4.D465   1984   394   84-7244
ISBN 0-8263-0737-X

Contents

Tables

Figures

Preface

This book is based on a report that I prepared for the Second National Commission on Marihuana and Drug Abuse, published in 1973 under the title *The Non-Western Use of Hallucinogenic Agents.* Subsequently, in 1976, it was published by the Sage Publishing Company in abbreviated form as *The Wilderness of Mind: Sacred Plants in Cross-cultural Perspective.*

Since 1969, my interest in the area of hallucinogens and culture has been sparked by the teaching of courses in this area at California State University, Fullerton, as well as by my field research in the coastal and Amazonian regions of Peru, where folk healers use hallucinogenic plants to treat emotional and psychological disorders.

A number of papers that I have written in the last fifteen years, several of which did not appear in the above volumes, have been incorporated into the text of this book. I would like to acknowledge those who have permitted me to use the following works: Dobkin de Rios 1970, 1972a, 1974a, 1975, 1976, 1977a, 1977b, 1979, 1982; Dobkin de Rios and Katz 1975; Dobkin de Rios and Smith 1977; Dobkin de Rios and Cardenas 1980; Janiger and Dobkin de Rios 1973, 1976; Katz and Dobkin de Rios 1971; and Emboden and Dobkin de Rios 1981.

Thanks are due to Dr. Carlos Alberto Seguin for his en-

ix

couragement and guidance during the fieldwork periods in Peru from June through August 1967 and from June 1968 through May 1969. I am also indebted for field support I received from the Foundations Fund for Research in Psychiatry (G67-395). I would also like to acknowledge the support of National Institute of Mental Health Post-Doctoral Fellowship MH05062, which enabled me to prepare the final draft of the 1976 Sage Publication while I was a fellow at the Medical Anthropology Program at the University of California, San Francisco.

It is my hope that the recurrent cross-cultural regularities that are observable among those societies using mind-altering plants will present us with a key to understanding and unlocking the doors of the art of prehistoric peoples, to reveal to us curious Westerners some of the belief systems of ancient peoples which are elusive in the archaeological record.

Part 1

Introduction

Chapter 1

Introduction

Various parts of plants, their vines, fungi, leaves, barks, and tubers, have served human beings as sources of food or twine. Some plants have also had a different impact on humans. These are the plants whose properties are mind-altering—that can, in some manner, change normal waking consciousness. In this study of the anthropology of sacred plants, I will examine societies ranging in complexity from the hunter-gatherer level to advanced civilization. It is my firm conviction, based on more than fifteen years of specialized study of hallucinogens and culture, that these substances have played more than a minor role in structuring the lives, beliefs, hopes, and values of large numbers of people. Members of preindustrial societies in many cultures with varying epistemological perspectives have always incorporated mind-altering plants into facets of daily activity. The economic behavior, the social organization, and the belief systems of some societies, for example, have been affected by the use of mind-altering plants. Until recently, however, little has been known about the cultural contexts in which these plants were used. Far too often, when anthropologists and early travelers deigned to discuss such plant use, they mentioned hallucinogens in an aside, a footnote, or without much interest or conviction. In part, this was due to the cultural biases of these

early scholars, travelers, missionaries, and botanists, most of
whom came from Europe and America. The attitudes in their
own societies toward the use of approved drugs such as alcohol
and tobacco did not adequately prepare them for a sensitivity
toward or awareness of the use of exotic plants, especially since
such matters were often shrouded in ritual secrecy. Recent re-
evaluations of the roles of mind-altering plants in non-Western
society have shown that their impact was much greater than has
generally been imagined (Harner 1968: 30).

This book will address itself to the use of mind-altering
plants, particularly hallucinogens in non-Western societies. Many
of the data have been culled from earlier publications that are
difficult to find. The book describes eleven societies in North,
Central, and South America, Asia, Africa, Australia, and New
Guinea. My own firsthand empirical research in Peru, where
plant hallucinogens are used in folk healing, will serve to illustrate certain thematic materials (Dobkin de Rios 1970, 1972a,
1972b, 1977a, 1977b). The contribution that anthropology can
make to the study of the use of mind-altering plants throughout
the world is to show how cultural variables such as belief systems, values, attitudes, and expectations structure one of the
most subjective experiences available to humankind.

Three major types of psychoactive drugs will be examined
and some discussion of their geographic distribution will follow.
Several themes emerge from the summaries of drug use. Plant
hallucinogens, whose antiquity in human history is greater than
generally recognized, have, for example, influenced human evolution. Shamanistic concepts and animistic beliefs that may be
influenced by the mind-altering properties of particular plants
will be discussed in specific cultural contexts. Another important
area that I will focus upon is the ways hallucinogenic drugs have
influenced ethical and moral systems.

I hope that this summary will prove useful in presenting a
series of empirically derived propositions worthy of future test-
ing. My attempt is to build a theory of drug effects that takes
into account the importance of antecedent cultural variables so
as to predict such effects.

Psychotropic Drugs

The term *psychotropic* has been used in scholarly circles as a synonym for the more popular term *psychedelic*. Psychotropic substances are those which cause psychological change or modify mental activity either by use of a plant or else by a chemical synthesis. The pharmacologist Delay (1967: 4) distinguished three broad types of psychotropic drugs, although within the following categories, we should note, there is considerable variation. The first group, the psychic sedatives, includes narcotics, barbiturates, and tranquilizers, many of which have been incorporated into modern psychiatric practice. In the second important group are the psychic stimulants (including amines), which are drugs of mood change. The third group, the psychic deviators, often called hallucinogens, are a category of great importance to anthropology because of their preponderance in non-Western society. They include numerous plants, as well as refined or synthetic substances such as LSD, psilocybin, mescaline, and harmine. Unlike the first category, hallucinogens do not cause physical addiction.

Studies of the chemical effects of hallucinogenic substances are many and outside the scope of this presentation (see Schultes and Hofmann 1973). Nonetheless, it is important to point out that although the unlettered shaman or medicine man in traditional society may have known much less than we do concerning the chemical action of such plants upon his clientele, he achieved great sophistication in the use of such plants many thousands of years prior to the discovery of the New World, or the European exploration of Siberia or Oceania.

Anthropologists are aware that chemical substances are by no means the only way that man has attempted to alter states of consciousness. Such activities as meditation, fasting, flagellation, exercise, trance induction, rhythmic dancing, and the like (often called psychotechnologies; see Tart 1975), have been used to vary the pace of everyday life and allow individuals to achieve contact with and control over preternatural realms. Ludwig (1969: 9) has written about the function of altered states in human societies, and their ubiquitous presence in some form or other bears witness to their cultural importance as well as their ability to satisfy both individual and social needs (see also Bourguignon 1973). The ingestion of hallucinogens has been a particularly rapid and reliable way to achieve an altered state of consciousness.

An initial study of the global distribution of hallucinogenic agents brings to light an interesting and, at first, puzzling finding. Hallucinogen use appears to have been more widespread in the Western Hemisphere than in Europe, Asia, or Africa. La Barre (1970) argues that the reason for such a difference can be found in the shamanism that plays such an important role in New World Indian society. The cultural value of personal revelation among successive waves of migrating PaleoIndian hunters led generations of such hunters to use and to experiment with whatever plant hallucinogens and stimulants could be encountered in their foraging.

In spite of gaps in the archaeological record, we can postulate that plant hallucinogens have very great antiquity. A Czech scholar, Pokorny (1970), has argued that plant hallucinogens are the key to understanding the stylizations and ornaments in paleolithic art from Prodmosti, Avjejeve, and Mozin in Czechoslovakia. Despite the fact that recorded history, too, contains major gaps, written records—such as the Vedic hymns of India, lauding the use of soma, and Homer's *Odyssey*—tell of the use of plants and other substances to alter consciousness. These plants were an important part of religious belief, used in both sacramental and social activity.

Plant hallucinogens may have played an important role in the evolution of *Homo sapiens* as a species. Certainly as human beings evolved from lower orders and posture became upright, the amount of land the species could cover for foraging increased and different varieties of wild plants were subject to scrutiny. Some of the psychotropic plants that were experimented with from early times might have stimulated language and communication about the unusual perceptions of reality that followed their ingestion. The advent of fire and the ensuing ability to boil substances may have permitted *Homo sapiens* to convert certain plants into a chemical state where their mind-altering properties were activated, for many hallucinogens must be pulverized, boiled long hours, or smoked in order to release their alkaloid properties.

As La Barre has shown, hunters and gatherers, rather than farmers, were probably the first to learn much about hallucinogenic plants. These people may have experimented with potential foodstuffs and narcotic plants as a source of revelation. Their neolithic descendants, who were abundantly supplied with staple cultigens and domesticated animals (at least in Old World societies) may have been less prone to experiment. As we will soon see from an examination of themes associated cross-culturally with drug use, mythological motifs concerning the role of animals in teaching man about plant hallucinogens tend to confirm this hypothesis.

Geographical Distribution of Psychotropic Plants

Although most hallucinogen-using societies are in the Western Hemisphere, this book will focus upon societies located in both the Old and New worlds. I will synthesize and assemble vignettes describing drug use, generally prior to European contact. By no means the only societies for which data are available, the groups described here can be augmented by others. I have focused in depth on a selected few in order to control comparisons. Because of the availability of data, I have chosen to examine

1. the Australian Aborigines of the central desert region,
2. the reindeer herdsmen of Siberia,
3. the Plains Indians of North America,
4. the Nazca fishermen of coastal Peru,
5. the New Guinean highlanders,
6. the Mochica of Peru,
7. the Maya of Mexico,
8. the Aztec of Mexico,
9. the Inca of Peru,
10. the Fang of northwestern equatorial Africa, and
11. Amazonian Mestizos.

Additionally, I have tried to control for factors of diffusion with the exception of Aztec influence on late Maya culture and

expected similarities between Nazca and Mochica cultures of
Peru. Of the eleven societies included in this book, analyses of
the ancient Maya, Nazca, Mochica, and Amazonian Mestizos
are the result of my own research (see Dobkin de Rios 1970,
1971, 1972a, 1972b, 1976, 1977b, 1978; Dobkin de Rios and Cardenas 1980).

The Importance of Cultural Variables

As various writers have pointed out, the hallucinogenic experience comprises an interacting set of variables such as the
attitude, expectations, motivation, mood, and personality of the
user, and the physical setting. The so-called psychedelic drug
experience is a complex one in which such interaction brings
forth one of the most subjective experiences available to psychological, sociological, or anthropological inquiry. For the most
part, hallucinogenic drugs present the subject with complex visionary content, which lasts from an hour or two to several. The
drugs' effects on perception and the individual's time sense are
quite unusual (see Ludwig 1969: 14–17), with time often perceived as slowing down or accelerating, or even seeming infinite
in its duration. The individual often experiences changes in perception, and emotions are heightened to reflect euphoria or
anguish. Powers of concentration, attention, memory, and judg-
ment are all affected. A person may either exhibit fear of losing
control as the effects of the plant take hold, or else (especially
if his culture so structures it), he may interpret such an experience as representing personal contact with godhead or divinity.
Body images undergo profound change, and distortions of one
sort or other are quite common. A schism may be felt between
body and mind, or else the opposite may occur, in that the
boundaries between man and the universe dissolve and the
individual reports experiences of unity with nature or godhead.
A sensation of synesthesia—the scrambling of sensory modalities—is an often reported effect of hallucinogenic ingestion. All
five senses are extremely heightened. People tend to attach special significance to their experiences, frequently reporting that
they experience a sense of the ineffable. In addition to the clinical

findings made by students of the phenomena (Barron et al. 1964; Barber 1970), another set of variables, cultural in nature, must be taken into consideration. Recent anthropological studies of modern, non-Western societies where hallucinogenic drugs are used for supernatural or medical goals point to the crucial role that cultural variables play in structuring what at first blush appears to be a purely subjective experience, lacking any cultural dimension. Nonetheless, as some writers have shown (Dobkin de Rios 1972b; Kensinger 1972), belief systems, values, and expectations do program the individual's subjective experience. My own work in the Peruvian Amazon points to the role that culture plays in evoking stereotypic visions among drug users. If we turn to the use of mind-altering drugs in Western society, we may find a contrast to this cultural patterning of visionary experience in traditional cultures. Lacking specific cultural traditions of drug use which program their experience, Westerners often report idiosyncratic patterns which actually are, in themselves, worthy of study.

The hallucinogenic experience can generate great anxiety on the part of the novice, in both traditional and industrial societies. The individual's anxiety may be allayed with the help of a "guide," whose role is an important one cross-culturally. To continue this metaphor, such a journey may require structuring by an outsider if it is to be as meaningful as possible. In traditional society, a guide's role is to bridge the two worlds of consciousness as a means of controlling and neutralizing perceived evil spirits that appear to the drug user during a session, as well as to evoke culturally expected visions. The guide generally uses music to accomplish these purposes. In part 3, I will examine in detail the relationship between music and hallucinogenic ritual.

Hallucinogenic Ritual and Theater

Anthropologists interested in hallucinogens and culture have often remarked privately upon the expressive elements in the hallucinogenic drug experience. These aesthetic elements have been reported in societies all over the world, from simple hunter/gathering peoples, pastoralists, and incipient agriculturalists, to members of ancient civilizations and folk segments of nation states. Cross-cultural expressive and theatrical dimensions of hallucinogenic rituals, as well as their instrumental functions, are important to consider.

The internal thespian flavor of the hallucinogenic journey can never be sensed by an impartial observer. Intrinsic to the effect of the drug is the power to evoke expressive experiences equal in force and drama to the best theater available anywhere. Unlike the urban theatergoer, however, who finds his way to a physical structure called a theater, in which actors give life to a script which another person has created in imitation of real events, the hallucinogenic questor experiences an entirely different genre of drama. In such drug rituals, the imbiber is actor, playwright, stage director, costumer, and make-up artist—even musician. Fast-moving, brilliant kaleidoscopes of colors, forms, patterns, and movement, more exotic than most people ever see in normal waking consciousness, are produced entirely from within the individual's psyche.

There is, however, in traditional societies, a stage manager for this hallucinogenic drama—the shaman/priest. Through music, chants, whistling, or percussion strokes, he evokes patterned visions that have specific cultural significance within the context of the ritual experience (see Katz and Dobkin de Rios 1971; Dobkin de Rios and Katz 1975).

My colleague Fred Katz and I have suggested that sudden access to the unconscious by means of hallucinogen ingestion, despite the aesthetic and expressive dimensions possible, is dangerous for human beings. Psychodynamically oriented researchers stress that the emotional response to such entry is displayed by the nausea, vomiting, diarrhea, tachycardia, and high blood pressure of the participant. Our early work pointed out that music, with its implicit structure, provides a substitute psychic structure during periods of ego dissolution. According to this hypothesis, music functions not merely to create mood within the drug setting. The shaman-guide creates—just as a stage director might—a corpus of music whose intrinsic structure provides the drug user with a series of paths and banisters to help him direct his visions during the actual experience, instead of becoming disoriented by the change in ego structure, anxiety, fear, and somatic discomfort brought on by the drug.

Shamans with whom I have worked claim that the music created during the drug experience provokes specific and highly valued drug visions. For example, music may evoke access to a particular supernatural entity (see part 2), or permit a vision which displays the source of witchcraft, suggests contact with ancestors, and so on. During most hallucinogenic drug ritual, there is little physical activity, although a few exceptions are recorded. Participants tend to be quiet and contemplative. However, sensory stimulants are consistently employed. Natural odors and plant perfumes, colorful body decorations, and tooth darkening are found. Percussive music is universal. Tactile stimulation comes from the close proximity of participants in group rituals, or from exorcism-like rituals of laying on of hands.

These rituals may be valuable because they provide a catharsis. Drugs work by creating an emotional abreaction similar to that felt by a Western audience who might witness a well-staged, well-written piece in a theater. Ludwig (1969) described the salient somatic and psychological effects associated with altered states of consciousness, many of which readily lend themselves to dramatic form. Especially in the area of emotional expression there seems to be a continuum of effects—the heavens and hells alluded to by Huxley (1954) in *The Doors of Perception*. Moreover, abreaction—a releasing of psychic tension through the acting out of a repressed traumatic experience—causes an appropriate emotion or effect to be felt by the individual, even when psychotherapeutic dynamics are not programmed into the hallucinogenic experience by a shamanic/priestly guide. Aristotle argued (1961: 9) that the aim of tragedy was to purge pity and fear: "The praxis that art seeks to reproduce is mainly a psychic energy working outwards." This commentary from ancient Greece can be illustrated from my work with *ayahuasca* (various *Banisteriopsis* spp.) in the Peruvian Amazon. In this setting, men and women sought the hallucinogenic experience to obtain visions, during which they saw before them the events of their bewitchment which they believed led to the onset of the diseases or misfortunes they suffered. The visions were the catalyst for shamanic ritual intervention, which signaled imminent cure through retribution directed toward the perpetrator of the evil.

This Amazonian psychic drama, without doubt, has been ritually reenacted elsewhere since time immemorial, inasmuch as throughout human prehistory illness has been thought caused by supernatural means (see Ackerknecht 1971). In those areas where plant hallucinogens have been used for healing, anteced- ent cultural variables in the form of specific beliefs provided the material from which interior scripts were designed (Dobkin de Rios 1975).

One additional area of interest to this discussion concerns the role of synesthesia, the experiencing of one sensory modality as another. Shamanic guidance of such experience entails stag- ing these interior dramas in natural settings with the use of a variety of odors, sounds, visual cues, and tactile aids to enhance the hallucinogenic effect. This aspect of synesthesia contributes to the overall dramatic effect of the drug experience.

The Shaman and Hallucinogenic Agents

Male shamans (generally regarded as technicians of the su- pernatural and also called medicine men or witch doctors) have always been magicians par excellence. Aided by the use of pow- erful hallucinatory adjuncts (as we see in the vignettes to be presented shortly), the magician could use his powers to cure patients, foresee the future, bewitch an enemy, obtain the favors of a desired woman, and, most important, to manipulate and control supernatural entities. The ethnobotanical literature is full of praise for the traditional or peasant shaman, whose knowl- edge of complex chemical substances is admirable. Certainly, such technicians have taken full advantage of the hallucinogens in their gardens and foraging areas in an attempt to open com- munication with supernatural realms as well as to tap resources within themselves.

The shaman, a specialist in techniques of ecstasy, is no stranger to those interested in the anthropology of religion. If we look at some major characteristics of shamanistic behavior throughout the world, we can associate much of this comportment with hallucinogenic plants. In fact, several shamanistic themes can be said to be influenced by the properties of hallucinogenic plants. These include such phenomena as the quest to obtain shamanic power, the presence of—or shaman's metamorphosis into— helping spirits or allies, the shaman's celestial journey or descent to the underworld, the often discussed magical flight or aerial voyage, the militaristic nature of shamanism, and the shaman's special healing abilities. In part 2, we will look in more detail at some of these themes linked to drug ingestion worldwide.

Eliade (1958) has viewed the shaman as a magician who attempts to control the unknown. His specialization is to enter into a trance state, during which time his soul leaves his body and ascends to the sky or descends to the underworld. Unlike people in possession states, a shaman controls special helping spirits with whom he communicates without ever becoming their instrument. The intensity of the shaman's experience is a theme that runs through most of the literature. Although scholars interested in shamanistic behavior frequently have not taken into account the role of hallucinogenic drugs in influencing such behavior, many of the properties of these drugs as discussed earlier may be implicated in shamanic activities.

Certainly, the visionary content of mind-altering drugs is unlike anything found elsewhere in life. The fast play of kaleidoscopic colors and forms, the realistic and fantastic aspects that appear, the change in sense perception, and the heightening of introspection all lend themselves to symbolic elaboration within the nexus of existing cultural beliefs. Although one might hesitate to join the small throng of enthusiasts who claim that such substances are the *fons et origo* of man's religious beliefs, their important influence on such belief systems throughout human history must not be discounted.

Hallucinogenic Drugs and Ethical and Moral Systems

To the Western observer of drug use in traditional society, a recurring theme is the "mana" or power that such plant hallucinogens are believed to possess. The mana itself, although neutral, can be directed by the drug user (either shaman or layman) to specific moral and ethical ends. At times, it is difficult to use a simplistic notion of good and evil as encapsulated in the Judeo-Christian tradition. As Herskovits pointed out (1946), such categorization is simply inapplicable to non-Western society. The shaman, in a pre-state-level society, is generally the moral arbiter of his community. His role is to redress wrongs to himself, his client, or the group to which he belongs. As a magician with access to and control over such powerful substances, he may use the power of the plant to cause death or to destroy an enemy's village. He may cure an illness or cause one for an adversary. The question of how such power should be used is a thorny one, although it is a recurrent concern in those societies where such plants are part of cultural patterns. To the Western observer, it often appears that a moral dilemma is posed in defining the nature of good and evil use of such drugs. My own data on *ayahuasca* use in the Peruvian Amazon indicate that informants clearly distinguish how plant hallucinogens should be properly used. Should they be employed to heal illness? to bewitch an enemy? to obtain the favors of a woman? to find out who stole a lost object? to divine the future? The alleged power of such plants obliges the user to make a decision on their use: should they be harnessed for one's own gain, prestige, psychological control over others; for self-aggrandizing behavior; to obtain the esteem of one's fellow men; or for particular pecuniary ends? Or, in contrast, should such substances be used for the benefit of the social group, to communicate with the spirit world so as to ensure the well-being of all members of the society? We find in traditional societies amalgams of community consciousness and individual shamanic powers.

As we will see in the vignettes to follow, peoples of the world have used hallucinogenic drugs in diverse cultural activities. Before we turn to specific case studies in order to examine the anthropological record in greater detail, it is important to note that the data available on such societies are often quite inadequate. Anthropologists, missionaries, botanists, and travelers, while leaving behind excellent records of material culture, have often failed us in the more esoteric sphere of symbols and beliefs. One writer, Richard Blum (1969), attempted a controlled study of drug use in non-Western societies. He utilized the Human Relations Area Files in an attempt to correlate data on drug use with social structure, material culture, and belief systems. Although over 250 societies were available for statistical analysis, the data were often so incomplete and inaccurate that the project yielded few major results.

This book, in contrast, will synthesize data from many sources other than the Human Relations Area Files, despite the fact that many sources are secondary. Moreover, there are gaps in the data that cannot be filled in or can only be filled by inference, where the cryptic comment of some European or American traveler leaves us tantalized about the place of hallucinogens in that society. Often travelers have dismissed possible data in a few sentences so that the more "interesting" customs (often of a sexual nature) could be presented. Only in recent decades in Western societies have anthropologists with a growing interest in mind-altering plants begun paying attention to the use of such plants among the people they study.

Turning to the ethnographies, we find that despite the incompleteness of the reports, the Australian Aboriginal tribes of the central desert region utilized a plant called pituri to facilitate social interaction, relieve hunger and thirst, divine the future, and pay for male circumcisions. We will look at the possible influence of the plant on belief systems and healing. The Siberian reindeer herdsmen used the fly agaric mushroom, which was interwoven with shamanic practices prior to European contact. The plant played a major role in permitting the herdsmen to communicate with supernatural realms for divination and achieving pleasurable effects.

The Plains Indians used various Nightshade plants and the mescal bean to achieve highly valued mystical states which brought contact with realms of the preternatural. In particular, their drug use brought intimate relationships between a warrior and a fierce wild animal in the hunter's vision quest.

Among the ancient Nazca fishermen of south coastal Peru, their rich heritage of ceramics and textiles allows us to reconstruct the role of the San Pedro cactus and the *wilka* shrub on their culture. Plant hallucinogens appear to have been used by regional religious and political leaders for control of political, psychological, and social arenas using the power made possible in drug-induced altered states.

The New Guinea highlanders, pig farmers and horticultur- alists, used mind-altering mushrooms quite differently from other peoples of the world who had access to mind-altering plants. Without any ritualization or ceremony, these highlanders en- gaged in running-amok behavior during part of the year under the effects of these plants. The New Guinea highlanders rep- resent a cultural anomaly in their nonritual use of plant drugs.

The Mochica of the north coast of Peru utilized the San Pedro cactus and various Nightshade plants as part of shamanic activities. Religious hierophants interwove good and evil, power and its manipulation and expression, and magical control over nature to serve their clients and the community.

The ancient Aztecs incorporated at least four major hallu- cinogenic plants into their pharmacopoeia, to serve their needs in sacrificing human victims, to entertain noble guests at cere- monial feasts, and for tributary payments. The drugs were also used in healing and bewitching, and by warriors to obtain cour- age to fight. We see in this society an interesting use of sacred plants for bellicose and aggressive purposes.

In Peru, among the ancient Inca, plant hallucinogens such as San Pedro, *wilka* snuff, and coca were not incorporated into cultural religious activities as elaborately as among the Aztec of Mexico. The Inca appear to have had a lesser interest in mind- altering plants than other New World civilizations, although the evidence indicates that drugs played an important role in folk healing, probably in the countryside.

The Fang peoples of northwest equatorial Africa, who ex- perienced the shock of French colonization, altered their tradi- tional use of the hallucinogenic plant *Tabernanthe iboga*. In the past, it was taken by these hunters and farmers to relieve fatigue and to aid in hunting, but in recent decades was incorporated into a religious revitalization movement called Bwiti, and given to initiates to enable them to experience firsthand the presence of the cultic divinity.

The ancient Maya in Preclassic times used hallucinogenic mushrooms, toad venom, and the rhizomes of the common water-lily plant. These substances influenced ancient Maya religion, especially in the areas of divination and healing.

In Peruvian Amazonian cities today like Iquitos and Pucallpa, men and women use the plant hallucinogen ayahuasca in the diagnosis and treatment of witchcraft-related illness. Folk healers assemble groups of patients several times a week and administer the plant potion to allow their clients to obtain visions of the men and women who bewitched them.

After the ethnographic vignettes of part 2, we will turn in part 3 to the themes of cross-cultural universality that emerge from the ethnographic data.

Part 2

Ethnographies

ple. Aside from some thirteen different species of native tobacco, which grew wild (Goodspeed 1954), the pituri plant was probably the most important plant used by these groups. Small doses of the plant, which contain the alkaloids scopolamine and hyoscamine, give rise to hallucinations and illusions. Detachment from time and space is another drug effect (Lewin 1964). Pituri was important in the social life of the Aborigines. Because it could quell hunger and thirst, not only did the plant make life tolerable in the desert but it enabled the Aborigines to travel long distances in search of the basic necessities of life. Its economic value to Aboriginal populations is attested by the presence of the so-called pituri roads, extensive trade networks that extended from the northern to the southern reaches of the desert area. They permitted the Aborigines to trade the plant (Spencer and Gillen 1899). Such items as spears, boomerangs, nets, shields, fish, and yams were exchanged for pituri by various tribal groups who lacked the plant in their own habitat (Basedow 1925). The roads crossed rivers and high mountain ranges. Pituri leaves were packed tightly into woven bags and traded over hundreds of miles.

The following uses of pituri have been cited in the literature:

1. It was given as a token of friendship to strangers (Johnston and Clelland 1933).
2. It was used as a pick-me-up and social comforter to foster feelings of friendship (Basedow 1925).
3. It was used in small water holes as bait to trap emus, parrots, and kangaroos (Spencer and Gillen 1899).
4. It was chewed as part of social interaction (Johnston and Clelland 1933).
5. It was used by old men who acted as seers, to obtain power and riches (Vogan 1890, cited in Johnston and Clelland 1933).
6. It was used as payment in circumcision and subincision rites (Horne and Aiston 1924).

The only form of written communication known to the Aborigines was linked to the trading of the pituri plant. Incised message sticks (see figure 2) made of wood were used by tribal

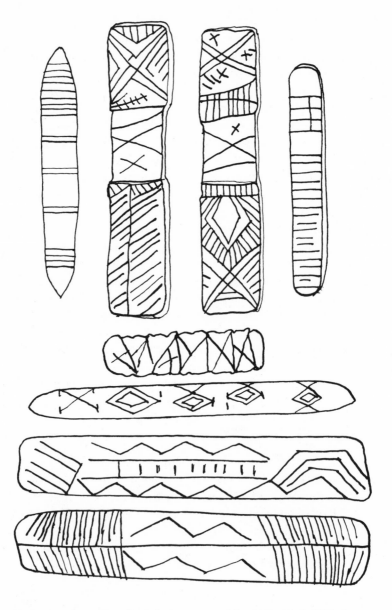

Figure 2. *Australian Aboriginal message sticks. (After Roth 1897: figs. 356–58)*

groups to indicate to neighboring tribes that they wanted to trade the plant. A complex sign language grew up relating to the substance, and old men sent message sticks to the owner of the commodity. This was somewhat like the use of a king's signet ring in medieval days, to show the genuineness of the king from whom the request was made (Roth 1897). A messenger carrying these special insignia would indicate what quantity of the plant he desired. The message sticks operated as a mnemonic device, since the notches and marks of different kinds were cut as aids to help the messengers recall their cargo. The sticks also functioned as safe-conduct in hostile territory (Spencer and Gillen 1899).

While no particular ritual activities were connected to the pituri plant, special magical rituals were invoked in connection with the acacia bush, called *wirra*. This substance was added to the pituri mixture, much as ash is added to the coca leaf in highland Peru today in order to release its alkaloid properties (Horne 1924).

With the advent of the Europeans and their introduction of processed tobacco, cigarettes slowly eliminated the use of pituri. By the 1950s, pituri was well on its way to extinction (Melvyn Meggitt, personal communication), and writers like J. C. Taylor (1977) could in clear conscience stress that Aboriginal medical systems were entirely without recourse to any pharmacologically active plant preparations. Today, there are only a few thousand Aborigines left in Australia. Many of their traditional customs are disappearing, as they move to reservations set aside for them or are assimilated into Western life-styles. Today pituri remains at best a dim memory of the past.

Although the influence of pituri on Aborigine belief systems is poorly documented, one can reasonably argue that the plant did indeed have an important role in Aboriginal religious life. Two factors can be cited to explain the absence of substantial data. For one thing, Aboriginal religious life, as Berndt (1964) and others have stressed repeatedly, was shrouded in secrecy. By the time Europeans generally became aware of pituri, they were merely chagrined that the plant killed livestock, rather than interested in its use within a tribal context. Moreover, by the

time anthropological studies of aboriginal populations were under way in this century, Aborigine culture was well into a state
of decline. These problems are common to other vignettes in
this book. As a result, only tentative suggestions can be offered
at this time concerning the influence of the pituri plant on Australian Aboriginal life.

As Eastwell points out in a series of recent papers on Australian Aborigines (1982, 1982b), the dominant white society has
accorded the Aborigines racist treatment since the time of contact. Because of the simple Aborigine social organization, the
Europeans found them hard to colonize. Their political system,
with power vested in the hands of elder men—which Europeans
described as gerontocracy—was unlike political systems in other
colonized areas. Like many other ethnic groups in the throes of
colonization, the Aboriginal population almost died out in the
nineteenth century. Usurpation of Aboriginal land and the diseases introduced by the Europeans accelerated the death rate
while the birth rate declined.

Fertility ceremonies have been historically widespread in
Aborigine culture. The goals of the ceremonies are to maintain
the group's well-being and increase population. Jones and Horne
(1972) described a recent Arnhem Land ceremony that took many
weeks of intensive preparation. Genital mutilations are commonly described in accounts of Aboriginal culture. Subincision,
which involves slitting the ventral surface of the penis to expose
the underlying urethra, has been discussed by a number of anthropologists. Explanations for this custom range from Bettelheim's psychoanalytic approach (1954) which suggests that this
was in response to envy of female menstruation, to others like
that of Cawte (1964), who argues that the genital alteration created a totemic likeness to the kangaroo bifid penis as well as to
the emu—two large mammals of summary importance in Aboriginal life. Aboriginal myth, Cawte argues, provides a social
charter for such affiliation between man and animals. Emu meat,
one of the main sources of animal protein available to Aborigines, was, interestingly enough, generally obtained not by any
special hunting techniques, but by luring emus to water holes
laced with pituri. The emus would become intoxicated and easy

to catch. The ritual identification of man with an animal by using a plant drug attractive to both is found elsewhere among drug-using peoples of the world (for example see chapter 3, below). Ritual mutilation of Aboriginal males to identify more closely with the emu or kangaroo is an interesting suggestion. Cawte points out that Aborigines see themselves as fully men—not as animal-men—and that their simulated likeness to the kangaroo or the emu merely affirms myths that charter association with animals. The genital mutilations, along with scarification and avulsion of the front teeth, are found in the context of teaching the myths to the initiate. The myths further provide, in a coded form, all sorts of information on the geographical location of vital water holes.

It is interesting that such a painful operation as subincision probably took place without the use of pituri, even though scopolamine is an excellent anesthetic. Its properties have been known and used by Westerners, and by the Second World War it was a widely used anesthetic in childbirth. While scopolamine did not eliminate pain, its soporific properties helped the patient to forget a surgical or childbirth trauma. Among the Aborigines who practiced painful genital mutilations on their young men, however, pituri was probably not used to dull pain. Recent studies on learning and memory show that heightened emotional states, in fact, augment learning (Bower 1981); pain may thus be a mnemonic aid in such a ceremony. In any event, the plant was recorded to have been used in payment for genital operations.

It is possible that a mystical relationship among man, plants, and animals, a recurrent totemic theme in Aboriginal culture, was reinforced by the use of pituri. It is quite likely that a plant such as pituri must have impressed the Aboriginal shaman and the initiate as a vehicle of communication with the supernatural world. It is also possible that the plant was used to induce trance and for divinatory purposes, which are widespread goals among other societies where hallucinogenic plants are used (see table 2).

Eastwell has argued that the Aborigines were familiar with spontaneous trancelike states (and probably those induced by drugs like pituri) and that trance states, which in modern times are regarded by Aborigines as illness, fall under the purview of native healers. Eastwell (1982) wrote of one informant who used the native term for *trance* to refer to the filaments secreted by an insect which are joined by the native healer to form a long string which is attached to the patient, and then to a nearby tree. This provides a track over which the patient's departed spirit can return. Eastwell points out that the word for *trance* has actually disappeared from Aboriginal language, which may be related to the disappearance of the pituri plant.

Diagnosis of illness within a framework of supernatural causation, too, may have owed something to the use of pituri. We do know, from only a brief reference in the literature, that pituri served as a revered totemic plant in Aboriginal society. Although its use must remain shrouded in speculation, it is quite possible that medicine men or mediums used pituri as a means of bridging the gap between the living and the departed. Although we shall perhaps never know the full extent of pituri's importance to the Aborigines, there is no doubt that they used and revered this hallucinogenic plant in several contexts.

Chapter 3

The Reindeer Herdsmen of Siberia

In the extreme northern and eastern regions of the Eurasian continent, the Siberian peoples have been herding reindeer in cold, wintry climates for many centuries. Since contact with the Russians in 1589, much of native culture has changed. In precontact times, however, the Siberian way of life differed immensely from that of their neighbors to the west, especially in that herds of wild reindeer were a most important source of food and skins. Owing to the vagaries of a pastoral existence in a severe climate where six-foot snow drifts last six months, these seminomadic pastoralists combined fishing and hunting with their herding activities. They used reindeer to draw sleighs long distances, and winter seasonal migrations were typical. The Siberians maintained an intimate relationship with their herds, paying particular attention to the breeding and foraging habits of these animals (Levin and Potapow 1956).

Despite differences in economic activities among Uralic-speaking peoples, most of the groups used the hallucinogenic mushroom *Amanita muscaria,* popularly called fly agaric, to alter states of consciousness. This fungus has over fifty different species, which occur in all continents except South America and Australia (Schultes 1970) and is found in a symbiotic relationship to the birch and fir trees. In recent years, the amateur mycolo-

Figure 3. Amanita muscaria. (*After Schultes and Hofmann 1973: 34*)

gists R. Gordon Wasson and his wife have written extensively of the use of this plant, not only among the Siberians (Wasson and Wasson 1957), but as the possible identity of the unknown *soma* of the ancient Hindus (Wasson 1968). Written historical accounts of the use of this plant begin in the seventeenth century, although we can assume that they mirror the process of culture change that led eventually to the Sovietization of the Siberian peoples, who were lured away from their indigenous drug use by amanita scarcity and by the introduction of commercially processed vodka. The best known Siberian tribesmen who used the mushrooms were the Chukchee, the Koryak, the Kamchadal, and the Yukagir.

In 1905, the American Museum of Natural History published a study of the tribes of the Maritime Provinces of Siberia and the extreme tip of Siberia, near Alaska. Two anthropologists, Jocelson (1905) and Bogoras (1910), who were members of the Jessup North Pacific Expedition, wrote about the fly agaric and how it was used. Generally, the plant was gathered during the month of August, when the characteristic crimson caps were in bloom. Only young girls could gather the plant and dry it. The Koryaks did not eat the mushroom fresh because they feared its toxic effects. Rather, they dried the plant in the sun first. Women were not permitted to eat the plant, although they were required to chew it and keep the quid in their mouths for a long time without swallowing it.

The alkaloids of fly agaric produce intoxication, hallucinations, and delirium. Other effects include the seeing of nearby objects either as very large (macropsia) or very small (micropsia). There can be movement and convulsions (Langsdorf 1809, cited in Wasson and Wasson 1957). Attacks of great animation alternate with moments of deep depression. *Amanita muscaria*, unlike most other hallucinogens, causes the user to exhibit great physical movement, which may be the source of the so-called ecstatic states of Siberian shamanistic seances. Before Siberians entered shamanic trances, they often consumed the plant. Many of the data on fly agaric, in fact, give us insight into traditional shamanic concepts, a large number of which are considered native to the Siberian peoples.

Of interest to the student of mushrooms is the importance of the use of the urine of an inebriate. The Koryak, for example, learned empirically that the hallucinogenic effects of the mushroom pass into a man's urine. As a result, men waited outside a house where the plant was being consumed in order to collect the urine of a user in special wood containers. The process was repeatable for five cycles before the drug began losing its potency. It is possible that the Siberian herdsmen learned about the relationship between the mushroom and its lingering effects in urine from their reindeer. When these animals eat lichens, they acquire a special longing for the urine of human beings. They frequent houses in order to drink men's urine. Every Koryak man carries a vessel made of seal skin, which he suspends from his belt as a container to catch his own urine. This is done as a means of attracting refractory reindeer. Sometimes, a reindeer will run to the camp from faraway pastures to drink urine-saturated snow, which appears to be a delicacy for them (Wasson and Wasson 1957). When reindeer eat the fly agaric mushrooms, which is not an infrequent occurrence, they behave in a drunken fashion, falling into a deep sleep. Steller (cited in Wasson and Wasson 1957) reported that if a Koryak encountered an intoxicated animal, he would tie its legs and not kill it until the drunkenness wore off. The Koryaks claimed that if one killed an animal while it was intoxicated, the effects of the fungus would be felt by all who ate the meat.

The *Amanita muscaria* mushroom has been used in several different ways by the Siberian reindeer herdsmen, generally by tribal elders (Jocelson 1905). The plant was used to facilitate communication with the supernatural, to divine the future, to diagnose the cause of illness, and for general enjoyment on festive occasions such as weddings, when it was offered to guests. On occasion, when the fly agaric was consumed, people asked questions of the person under the plant's intoxication, which he may have answered sensibly. The answers were based on the imbiber's visions.

The Koryak believed that the mushroom was endowed with particular power. Harmful beings, called *nimvits*, were believed to be controlled only by shamans. Communication with these beings took place only at night, in total darkness, by use of the plant. After the shaman consumed the mushroom, he fell into a trance. When the shaman awoke, he would relate his visions to those around him, often reporting that he entered into the next world and arranged meetings with dead kinsmen who instructed him. However, all men could eat the fungus, whether or not they were shamans, to find out why they might be ill, to explain a dream, or merely to reveal aspects of the upper or lower universe. The Koryak believed that when a person is intoxicated by the plant, he does what the spirits who reside within the plant tell him to do.

Groups like the Chukchee believed that the mushrooms actually constituted another "tribe." Intoxication brought to the user visions in the form of men. In effect, the visions personified the mushroom, and the "mushroom men" who appeared were as many as the number of plants consumed. These creatures were believed to take a person under his arms and accompany him on a voyage through the world. These mushroom men show the inebriate some real things as well as many unreal apparitions. The creatures follow intricate paths and like very much to visit places where the dead reside (Bogoras 1910).

Among the Yurk Samoyed, the forest magicians knew the custom of eating fly agarics when they were dry and fully grown. If an intoxicated man did not view the mushroom spirits properly, they could kill him. Like the Chukchee, these people reported man-like creatures who appeared before them in a dream. The creatures promptly ran away along the path which the sun travels after it has set in the evening, so that it can rise again. An intoxicated person once followed closely behind these spirits, according to one writer (Lehtisalo, cited in Wasson and Wasson 1957), since the spirits run slowly. Along the journey, the fly agaric spirits tell a man what he wants to know, such as whether he will be able to cure a sick person. When the individual came out into the light again, he found a pole with seven holes and cords. He then tied up the spirits and awoke. He sat down, took in his hand a symbol of the pillar of the world—a four-sided staff with seven slanting crosses cut into each side at its upper end—and sang about what he heard in his journeying.

In discussing the religion of the Ugrian folk peoples, Karjalainen (1927, cited in Wasson and Wasson 1957) wrote of *Amanita muscaria* intoxication. He stressed that when the mushrooms were eaten in an ordinary manner, various precautionary rules were invoked because of their toxicity. However, when a shaman eats the mushroom, the act takes on cultic significance. This is so because by eating the mushroom the shaman creates helpers for himself. Among the Vasyugan tribe, according to Karjalainen (ibid.), music played an important part in the mushroom ritual. Magicians attempted to communicate with the spirits and obtain the information they needed, sometimes using dream visions, enhanced by the mushrooms, in divining the future.

Another Siberian group, the Ostyaks, had varying fly agaric ceremonies. A hut was filled with the smoke of a resinous tree bark. A shaman took three to seven fly agaric caps, after fasting all day, and then slept for a while. Afterward he rose, shouting, walking about, his body trembling with excitement, to report what the spirit was revealing to him through his emissaries. The mushroom told him which spirit would be propitiated, how to regain good luck, and so forth. After these emissaries had told everything and left, the shaman would sink into a deep sleep until morning.

The shaman's traditional costume exemplifies aspects of shamanic practices and the value of the teachings of the reindeer about the fly agaric mushroom. In former times, Siberian shamans used to appear in complete animal disguise, with fur covering their bodies and antlers on their heads. Such symbolic dress may have signified the debt of the shaman to the humble reindeer, whose delight in human urine may have been the vehicle through which knowledge about augmenting drug effects in human beings was acquired.

The Wassons, in their monumental two-volume book *Russia, Mushrooms and History* (1957), discuss the use of the fly agaric as an inebriant dating back to perhaps 10,000 years before present; in their analysis, *Amanita* use began at the end of the Ice Age. They argue that the virtues of this plant were probably discovered rather early in human prehistory, as the mushroom co-occurs with the birch and pine trees, both of which spread over the Siberian plains soon after the retreating ice cap. Although much of the anthropological testimony cited by the Wassons and discussed in this section attests to the value that the plant had in Siberian reindeer hunting societies, it is probably true (as the Wassons point out) that many of the observers who paid attention to the cult did so in its dying phase when the integrity of beliefs in the plant had been undermined. Altaic-speaking groups, who displaced the fly-agaric-using tribes, did not themselves consume the red-speckled mushroom, although it is possible that they absorbed into their shamanic practices a series of beliefs associated with the use of the mushrooms. As we will see throughout this book, many belief systems connected with the use of a particular drug exist in neighboring communities where the drug itself may not have been used. Nonetheless, we must not overlook the importance of such similarities among various hallucinogenic drugs, which account for the similarity of symbolic patterning from society to society and hence for the repetition of certain themes over and over in the literature. More about this in part 3.

We should note that Eliade (1958) disagreed with the Wassons, arguing that hallucinogenic drug use in Siberia is a degradation of the original states of ecstasy reported for shamans; in 1973, however, Eliade moderated his arguments somewhat. In arguing that native peoples have used plant products extensively to heighten their shamanistic activities, writers like the Wassons suggest the great resourcefulness of nonliterate peoples, who have discovered the amazing properties of the plants available in their environment and have learned how best to prepare and utilize these substances.

Chapter 4

The Plains Indians of North America

The Plains Indians, who lived in the region ranging from the foothills of the Rocky Mountains to the eastern woodlands and south to Mexico, were nomads who exploited a vast land area in search of grazing animals, particularly the bison. These animals provided clothing, shelter, and food. Horses, which came north from Mexico where the Spanish explorers had brought them in the sixteenth century, radically changed the culture of the Plains Indians. Although some tribal groups practiced mixed hunting and horticulture, their dependence upon large animals was of paramount importance to their culture.

These tribal groups used a few powerful hallucinogenic plants in their religious ceremonies, including various Nightshade plants, the mescal bean, and tobacco. As it was throughout North American Indian societies, personal revelation was highly valued among Plains Indians. Drug plants played an important role in helping individuals to achieve heightened states in which they felt that supernatural revelation was available to them.

Plains Indians took advantage of the few hallucinogenic flora available in their habitat. Although peyote eventually diffused to the North from Mexico in historic times, two major plants were used, in addition to tobacco, before the contact period. They were the jimson weed (*Datura stramonium*; see

fig. 4) and the mescal bean (*Sophora secundiflora;* see fig. 5). Datura
was used by many southwestern Indian groups, including those
in Arizona, New Mexico, Texas, and California. An early Spanish
writer, Hernández, wrote that the fruit of one of the Datura
plants, *D. stramonium,* could cause insanity if eaten incautiously
(cited in Safford 1915).

Tobacco Use Among Plains Indians

Tobacco played an important role in Plains culture. Although all Plains tribes probably smoked tobacco, not all cultivated the plant. The Cree and the Comanche, for example,
obtained tobacco in trade. Among the Crow, who could obtain
the seeds of the plant with difficulty, the young tobacco society
novice would learn to interpret his dreams in such a way as to
help him decide on a propitious place to plant the seeds to ensure
a good harvest (Lowie 1954). (Only men smoked the *Nicotiana
rustica.*)

Since the wild ancestors of the tobacco plant do not exist in
North America, we know that tobacco use on this continent
diffused from contact with South America. One species used
among the Plains tribes was *Nicotiana attenuata,* which is found
as far north as western Canada. Several other plants were often
mixed with tobacco; it is possible that some strains were more
potent than others.

Tobacco was not perceived by the Plains Indians as a secular
plant, although we think of it as such. Plains medicine bundles
almost always contained a pipe and tobacco; it was believed that
sacred objects in the medicine bundle could help an individual
establish rapport with the supernatural. Pipes were passed around
at council meetings and were especially important during peace-
making ceremonies. Tobacco was also burned as incense or cast
into the air or onto the ground (Driver 1961). Shamans used the
plant to establish contact with their spirit helpers and to drive
disease away from a patient's body.

Native American Indian use of tobacco parallels the use of
other substances that are known to produce hallucinogenic effects (Janiger and Dobkin de Rios 1973). Such Indian groups

Figure 4.   Datura stramonium. (*After Heiser 1969: 138*)

were very pragmatic and somewhat parsimonious in their approach to plant drug use. Recent investigations on the chemical nature of tobacco smoke and its biological effects, as well as the background literature on the tribal use of *Nicotiana* species by New World traditional societies prior to European contact, provide the stimulus to reexamine this intriguing issue.

Harmala alkaloids—harman and norharman—have recently been isolated from cured commercial tobaccos and their smoke (see Cuzin 1967; Poindexter 1962a, 1962b; Testa and Testa 1965). They constitute a chemical group—the Beta carbolines—of which several closely related members with similar pharmacological properties have been found to be hallucinogenic (harmine [Lewin 1928; Pennes and Hoch 1957], harmaline, tetrahydroharmine, and 6-methoxy harmine [C. Naranjo 1967]). Although native varieties of tobacco and tobacco preparations have not yet been analyzed for Beta carbolines, it is reasonable to assume that concentrations of these substances may vary widely depending upon the conditions of cultivation and growth. The amounts of tobacco taken may further concentrate the harmala alkaloids.

Previous work with harmine by Davis et al. (1969, 1970) indicates that relatively small doses of this substance cross the blood-brain barrier and change neural transmission in the visual system. Recent work by these same investigators would seem to indicate that similar concentrations of harman may produce comparable effects.

Nicotine, the most potent agent in tobacco smoke, has been subject to scientific investigation for a great many years. However, its effects on the central nervous system are just beginning to be explored. It has been found that nicotine may affect the concentration of biogenic amines in the brain, particularly serotonin, whose chemical structure is similar to that of LSD. This chemical may predispose a person to changes in consciousness, although its effect would ordinarily be masked by the initial autonomic effects of nicotine in the average smoker (see Murphree 1967). It has further been shown that Vitamin B6 metabolism is altered through smoking, with a subsequent depletion of the vitamin. This in turn may contribute to mental changes in the smoker (El-Zoghby et al. 1970).

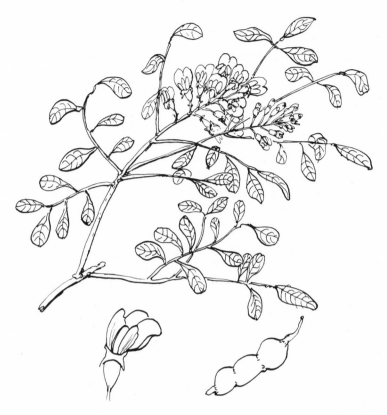

Figure 5.   Sophora secundiflora. (*After Schultes 1970*)

One botanist, Heiser, has argued that the tobacco the New World Indians smoked was a far cry from the mild blends, such as Virginia tobacco, used today in the cigarette industry in the United States and Europe. As Heiser said (1969: 161) and as tables 1–4 show, tobacco "literally knocked the Indians out." He stated that "any plant that had the power to induce a strong narcotic state and allow the user to have hallucinations would have been significant to primitive man."

The data presented below on the New World aboriginal use of tobacco, although by no means all-inclusive, should provide a useful validation of the recent chemical data on tobacco smoke condensates and their probable hallucinogenic properties.

Tobacco Use in New World Prehistoric Societies

Tables 1–4 are organized thematically to treat North American man's use of tobacco in the pre-European contact period. The data are categorized according to the following scheme: 1) nondivinatory magico-religious use; 2) divination; 3) healing; 4) pleasure, social interaction, and fortitude. Whenever possible, data were obtained on the period prior to the European reintroduction of the tobacco plant to minimize possible effects of acculturation. It should be noted that although the categories in tables 1–4 are cognitively distinct for the Western reader, disease etiology, prognosis, and cure cannot be separated from preternatural realms in much of non-Western society.

As these tables indicate, tobacco was not only smoked, but taken in decoctions, salves, and wads. Heiser (1969) mentions in a summary statement that the Plains peoples used the tobacco plant as a medicine for all sorts of disease, as a protection against evil spirits, as a powerful agent against a warrior's enemies, for magic in hunting, and as a means of communication with the gods. Several early descriptions emphasize the great part ceremony and ritual played in Plains tobacco use.

If, indeed, tobacco is a hallucinogenic agent, then its use should be culturally patterned in a way similar to that of other psychotropic substances. We may draw an analogy for the Plains peoples from data gathered in South America, where many *mon-*

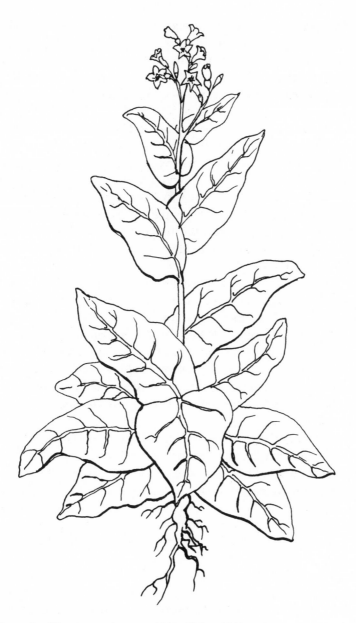

Figure 6. Nicotiana tabacum. (*After Heiser 1969: 158*)

43

taña tribes in the Amazonian region used tobacco smoke to induce trances, dreams, and visions. Tobacco smoke served as an
important adjunct to shamanistic techniques. The personal revelation of the preternatural was highly regarded throughout New
World Indian societies and any plant which helped to alter states
of consciousness and permit communication with spirit forces,
such as the smoke from tobacco, would likely have been eagerly
incorporated into an already rich pharmacopoeia.

Wallace's early work in this area (1959) has shown the crucial
role that culture plays in determining the patterning of visionary
and drug-induced trance states. Wilbert reopened the question
in 1972 and made clear that among the Warao Indians of Venezuela not only is tobacco used functionally as if it were a hallucinogen, but cultural goals determine the style of visionary
ecstatic experience.

The role of cultural variables such as expectation, belief
systems, and values is of paramount importance in understanding how one of the most subjective of human experiences can
take on cultural direction. The reader, drawing on his own tobacco-
smoking experiences or those of others around him, may scoff
at the notion that tobacco smoking could be labeled hallucinogenic activity. Nonetheless, if we postulate the following based
on chemical and anthropological data, our conclusions are in
order:

1) The evidence cited in tables 1–4 and recent chemical findings suggest that the peripheral autonomic effects of nicotine in
tobacco would not be those sought after by traditional societies
for magico-religious, divinatory, or ceremonial use.

2) Variations in species potency due to variables of climate,
soil composition, and so forth may explain reported differences
in experiences with consciousness alternations from *Nicotiana*
use.

3) A series of intervening cultural variables is crucial in situations where alterations in consciousness are valued and expected. Although there have been no controlled studies of the
possible consciousness-altering effects of tobacco smoking in human beings, this may be due to several factors: a) the effects
hypothesized may not have been specifically sought after; b) the

Table 1. Nondivinatory magico-religious use of tobacco.

Cultural Use	Society	Reference
Improve fishing, abate storms and lightning, or thanksgiving for escape from danger	Caroline Indians; Seminoles	Koskowski (1957: 66)
Offerings of tobacco to supernatural spirits or gods	Iroquois; NW Venezuela tribes; Indians E of Rocky Mts.; Maya	Fenton (1940: 426), Steward (1949: 21), Koskowski (1957: 68), Thompson (1970: 112)
Augment magical properties of body; tobacco smoke or snuff used in boys' initiation ceremonies at puberty	Yibaro, Rio Pasteza Maya Tucuna Indians	Koskowski (1957: 69) Thompson (1970: 108) Metraux (1949: 377)
Transmit spirit of courage and fearlessness as essential qualities for overcoming foe	Caribs, Brazil	Koskowski (1957: 70)
Tobacco, boiled in water or steeped, taken through mouth and drunk, to narcoticize drinker, usually shaman; preparation for shamanhood	Montaña tribes, Peru; Jivaro, Zaparo	Cooper (1949: 534–43)
Smoked to induce trance, dreams, and visions; communication with spirits by shaman	Montaña tribes, S American rain forest; Warao, Venezuela	Cooper (1949: 534) Wilbert (1972: 55–56)
Obtain visions, as unbreakable rule for action	Guayupe, E Andes	Steward (1949: 35, 390)
Offering to great deity, placed on grave boxes	Menomini Indians	Hoffman (n.d., cited in McGuire 1898: 568)
Used to insure hunting success	Tewa, San Ildefonso Omaha Indians	Whitman (1940: 402) Long (1823, cited in McGuire 1898: 568)

Table 1, continued.

Cultural Use	Society	Reference
Smoking, to provoke visions of *arutama* and other spirits; to give young boys advice; conjure up spirit of tobacco and transfer its power to boy; to make him brave, successful warrior; to kill many enemies or give individual hunting skills	Jivaro, E Ecuador	Karsten (1935: 293–94, 241–42)
Used ceremonially to please and nourish rain gods so that they will make sacred cloudflow drop rain on earth	Tewa, San Juan	Laski (1958: 140)
Religious emphasis on magical power of smoke to ward off evil	Tarahumara, Mexico Maya	Bennett and Zingg (1935: 45), Landa (cited in Thompson 1970: 120)
Smoked in forked tube as holy activity	Haiti (Hispaniola)	Oviedo (1535, cited in Brooks 1938: 202)
Used in ointment with Ololiuhqui, to communicate with their "Devils"	Aztecs, Mexico	Acosta (1590, cited in Brooks 1938: 310)
Used to honor Huitzilopochtli, God of War	Aztecs	Thompson (1970: 121)

Table 2. *Divination by means of tobacco.*

Cultural Use	Society	Reference
Smoking to see spirits that predict the future	Yíbaro, Rio Pasteza	Koskowski (1957: 69)
Smoke used in shamanistic divination, watching direction in which smoke drifts	NW Venezuelan tribes; Florida Indians; Goajiro, Colombia	Steward (1949: 21), Liebault (1579, cited in Brooks 1938: 289), Nicholas (1901, cited in Cooper 1949: 535)
Smoking before going to war to foresee the future	Cumana Indians, N of Orinoco River	Kirschoff (1949: 489)
Tobacco juice used by priests to work up madness (with other ingredients) and fury to receive the "Devil's" oracle	Aztecs, Mexico	De Solis (1724, cited in McGuire 1898: 372)
Smoking to produce dreams to offer flourishing of gardens and well-being of livestock	Jivaro, E Ecuador	Karsten (1935: 116)
Smoke used to make oneself drunk to see visions, to know of future success, and for "deception of Devil"	West Indian groups	Monardes (1571, cited in Brooks 1938: 249)
Smoking to learn of future events and consult on request and petition of others	Maya	Fuentes and Guzman (cited in Thompson 1970: 115)

47

Table 3. Tobacco and the treatment of disease.

Cultural Use	Society	Reference
Ward off evil spirits (*sespes*) that cause insomnia	Cahuilla Indians, California	Koskowski (1957: 73)
Purge superfluous steam and other gross humors	Roanoke Island Indians, Virginia	Harriot (1585, cited in Fairholt 1859: 23)
Used with elder leaves, fried in butter, as salve for wounds	Cherokee Indians	Hohman (1820, cited in Vogel 1969: 37)
Leaves applied to insect bites and stings	Maya	Vogel (1969: 217)
Tobacco wad, placed inside tooth cavity	Iroquois, New York	Speck (cited in Vogel 1969: 247)
Used with other herbs to treat diarrhea; combined with salt and pepper as abdominal purge in recurrent disease	Aztecs	Badianus (MS, cited in Vogel 1969: 381)
Used to cure headache and dysentery	Jivaro, Conibo, Campa, Piro, Peru	Cooper (1949: 535)
As main diagnostic procedure, to induce trance by decoction of tobacco	Widespread through South American Indian groups	Cooper (1949: 626)

48

Table 3, continued.

Cultural Use	Society	Reference
Smoked by shaman in gigantic cigar, to fumigate patient	Widespread, from Caribbean Islands to Tierra del Fuego	Cooper (1949: 626)
Treatment of rheumatism, humors, and pains in head	Venezuelan Indian groups	Herrera (1726, cited in McGuire 1898: 403)
Used in native surgery and in case of any hurt	West Indies	Knevet (1705, cited in McGuire 1898: 405)
Fumigation of muscle ache	Tapirape, Brazil	Wagley (1943: 57)
Ensure good health by smoking	Iroquois, Montreal	Cartier (1545, cited in Brooks 1938: 209)
Smoking to enter trance state and obtain visions from council of Gods, used to cure	Haiti (Hispaniola)	Benzoini (1565, cited in Brooks 1938: 226)
Ward off evil influence of disease	Seminoles; Yibaro, Rio Pasteza	Koskowski (1957: 67, 69)

Table 4. Tobacco, pleasure, social interaction, and fortitude.

Cultural Use	Society	Reference
Various hedonistic ends	Diverse West Indian groups	Cooper (1949: 527, 534)
To relieve fatigue and weariness	Tapirape Indians, Brazil San Salvador Groups	Cooper (1949: 535) Las Casas (cited in Brooks 1938: 243)
To avert hunger and thirst	Florida Indians	Laufer 1924 (cited in Blum 1969: 89)
Used in the course of everyday life	Bahama River Caribs	Gillin (1936: 66)
Smoking in councils of war; to fortify oneself against one's enemies	Carib Indians, Brazil	Thevet (1558, cited in Brooks 1938: 217), Lery (1578, cited in Brooks 1938: 283)
Tobacco pipe given quarreling men, to achieve harmony	Plains Indians, U.S.	La Barre (1970: 143)

effects may be greatly variable and dependent upon the setting, the personality of the smoker, the quality of the tobacco, the amount taken, and the culturally determined expectations of its use; c) the effects of harman and norharman may be cumulative, with a greater propensity for these effects in chronic smokers.

Jimson Weed

In addition to tobacco, several plants belonging to the Datura species, called jimson weed in English and *toloache* in Spanish (from the Nahuatl language of the Aztecs), were used by numerous Plains tribes. They contain a large amount of tropane alkaloids, which are highly toxic and include atropine, hyoscyamine, and scopolamine (Heiser 1969). No doubt the Plains Indians who experimented with this plant realized its potent properties very early. When this plant was used, the Indians believed it to be so powerful that they used it only to a limited extent for certain ceremonies. The plant was taken when someone wished to locate a thief, or to revenge unrequited sexual advances. Datura was used only by one individual at a time, and little actual ritual was connected to its ingestion. If someone's property had been stolen, a search would begin. A man either chewed some of the jimson weed or drank some of it in a solution. If a person was in poor health, he might not chance taking the powerful plant himself, but prefer to hire a substitute to take the plant in his place.

Three different types of narcotic effects were reported associated with Datura, occurring in the same individual on different occasions depending upon his sensitivity. Trance, visionary experience, or audible hallucinations could all occur. Sometimes a person might experience two or even all three effects. When the individual entered into trance, he wandered about in a stupor or partial narcosis. During his wanderings, it was said that he would find the thief or locate his lost or stolen articles. If he had a visionary experience, it would indicate the location of his property or the identity of whoever stole it. If this did not occur, the person seemed to know where to look when the drug effect terminated. Voices might appear and direct the person to the hiding place. To native informants, these effects were proven time and again. The Plains Indians believed explicitly that the visionary properties of the plant helped them to find vanished goods. Not only did informants cite instances of recoveries that they had made, but also several instances when individuals accused of theft subsequently confessed (Safford 1916).

The visionary effects of jimson weed were also used to diagnose illness. If a taboo was violated, or if an animal or person was responsible for causing an illness, all would be revealed to the drug taker. Once a cause was established, particular chants could be called upon in order to effect a cure. The leaves of the rest of the jimson weed were used medicinally to treat internal sores or internal injuries. On rare occasions, it was given with tobacco to treat delirium. Hill (1938) reported one informant who made a sacrifice to the plant and then drank a solution made from it which he claimed cured him of a hernia-type illness.

The Mescal Bean Cult

A lesser known drug, first described by Ortega in 1798 (see Howard 1957), was an evergreen shrub, or small tree, bearing bean-like scarlet seeds. The mescal bean, as it was called, was used by various North American Indians, including the Plains Indians, because of its hallucinogenic properties. When ground up in a powder, it was often taken in a drink made from the agave plant, also called the mescal; hence the associational name "mescal bean." Along the Mexican border, the beans were highly valued. A string of them measuring six feet in length would be accepted in exchange for a pony (Safford 1916). Only half a bean produced a delirious exhilaration, followed by a deep sleep lasting two to three days. It was reputed that ingestion of an entire bean could kill a man.

These mescal beans were widely known many miles on either side of the Mexican border area. Archaeological data show that mescal beans were in use in at least twelve cave and rock-shelter sites in southwest Texas for several thousand years (Campbell 1958). The sixteenth-century Spanish writer Cabeza

expedition, a horse could be exchanged for eight or ten of the beans (Schultes 1960). The plant was associated with first fruit rites, and often taken before buffalo meat, green corn, or pumpkin was eaten. In the late nineteenth century when peyote came into general use among several southwestern Indian groups, one would occasionally find the mescal beans boiled in a tea along with the peyote buttons. Some of the old timers liked to mix the medicines, although many did not.

The Pawnees had a society known as the Deer Dance Society in which the mescal bean played a prominent role. It was taught that all animal powers were learned through visions given by the mescal bean. The cult dancers imitated many kinds of animals. In the initiation ceremony, a candidate was given a tea made from the mescal bean. He would fall unconscious, and was subjected to a test of physical prowess, during which time the effects of the bean were supposed to anesthetize him. Shamanistic feats were often performed in regular ceremonies through the use of this plant. It is interesting to note that the regular ceremony of the Deer Dance Society occurred only when the wild sage plant reached a certain stage of maturity. As in other parts of the non-Western world where plant drugs are used in ceremonial activity, olfactory adjuncts are crucial to ensure a nonfrightening experience for the initiate. When the sage plant was mature, it was spread thickly around the lodge and used in incense offerings (Murie 1914 cited in Howard 1957).

The Wichita tribes also used the mescal beans in their ceremonies and were responsible for the diffusion of the cult to northern tribes. A dance was held three or four times a year, when grass had just appeared or when corn was either ripe or harvested. A novice was given a small red bean that produced a violent spasm, making him fall to the ground unconscious. He was thus believed unable to suffer pain when the jaw of a garpike was drawn over his naked body. During the ceremony, offerings were made to different deities. Those who took part in the ceremony generally vomited violently afterward. At the end of this ritual and after a feast, there was a ceremonial foot race, in which all members of the tribe—men as well as women—competed. The purpose of the foot race was to build up endurance for those who would go on the warpath. It was believed that the ceremony had the effect of removing all evil influences from the camp and promoting good health, long life, and general prosperity (Dorsey 1904 cited in Howard 1957).

One of the interesting uses to which the mescal bean was put by the Wichita was to enable a novice to enter a trance, during which time he would usually hold a conversation with some fierce wild animal who instructed him to be brave and to be a good warrior. Animals of this sort were believed to possess magical powers and acted as the guardians of the medicine men. The power thus obtained from the mescal bean rite was used in healing. The songs a man would sing during the medicine men's ceremony told of his particular experience with the animal (ibid.).

The last known mescal bean ceremony among the Wichita was performed in 1871. The only ones permitted to participate were medicine men, each of whom possessed his own songs or song, which described the origin of his magic power.

Howard (1957) has summarized the two principal forms of the mescal bean cult. The first type, practiced by the Iowa, Omaha, Oto, Pawnee, Wichita, and probably the Comanche and Delaware, resemble the Grand Medicine Lodge of the Central Algonquin tribes. The shaman would magically shoot mescal beans, aided by the wearing of a costume of animal skins with deer symbolism prominent. A second form, practiced by the Apache, Ponca, and Tonkawa, resemble the modern peyote ritual. Both cults utilized the mescal bean in a narcotic drink for its members and both featured magical performances by shamans. Since mescal beans were used as part of the ornamental dress of the peyote ceremony's leader in recent years, some writers have argued that the mescal bean cult was a substitute for peyotism, but there is good evidence that the mescal cult was the forerunner of peyote ceremonialism in the southwest Plains.

Belief Systems

Both Datura and the mescal bean fit well into the Plains Indian world view. Well known among the Plains Indians was

the vision quest (Benedict 1922), which involved fasting, isolation, and self-mutilation over several days. The goal was to
achieve contact with a guardian spirit, whom the future warrior
could call upon in times of difficulty. Such spiritual contact was
renewed periodically during the warrior's lifetime (Spencer et
al. 1965).

Shamans, too, played an important part among Plains Indians. They were seen as direct intermediaries between man
and the supernatural, and their activities included helping others
to achieve this highly desired contact for themselves. Shamans,
for example, instructed young men in ritual preparation for the
vision quest. In stratified societies the bureaucratization of religious activity serves as a substitute for direct revelation. Plains
Indian shamans, in contrast, instructed, taught, or guided the
young toward the correct path of personal ecstatic learning.
Some shamans could foretell the future and predict the location
of bison herds or indicate the future success of a war party.

Chapter 5

The Nazca Fishermen of Coastal Peru

On the south coast of Peru, an ancient people called the Nazca left a rich heritage of ceramics, textiles, and metalworks as testimony to the complex social and cultural achievements of their time (c. A.D. 100–800). While a large archaeological and interpretative literature exists to evaluate the Nazca way of life and world view, none of the studies attempts to understand the role of the plant hallucinogens they commonly used. This chapter will focus first on Nazca ceramic art as a source of symbolism and imagery related to the use of hallucinogens in the context of the Nazca economy and religious ceremonialism. The Nazca employed the plant hallucinogens *Trichocereus pachanoi*, a cactus; coca (*Erythroxylon coca*); Datura species; and the *wilka* snuff, *Anadenanthera peregrina*. These and other psychoactive substances are used in Peruvian healing throughout the coast and tropical rain forests today, and appear to have been in continuous use through prehistoric periods.

The massive earthworks known as the Nazca "lines" may in fact have been the portrayal by religious shamanic leaders and their followers of power symbols and icons. Such leaders were enmeshed in a world view focusing on power and dominion of man over nature. In other societies where plant hallucinogen use is common, shamans believe that they are able to transform

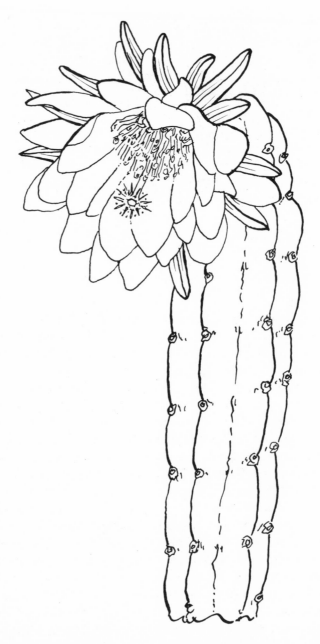

Figure 7. Trichocereus pachanoi. (*After Emboden 1979a: 65*)

themselves into a series of fish or animal familiars (see chapter 7, below). I believe that this was the case among the ancient Nazca, and in this chapter I will examine the multifaceted role of the shaman as hierophant of society. Since he was responsible for the fecundity of the earth and its creatures, and his function was also a combative one—in opposing negative forces that threatened his community—his political/religious role was that of a guardian/psychopomp, and was probably enhanced by the power that he and his followers believed was inherent in plant hallucinogen ingestion. Survival was difficult for the Nazca, since fresh water was hard to obtain in their harsh environment, and their ceramic art reflects preoccupation with survival, fecundity, and continuation of natural resources by means of shamanic plant hallucinogen use.

Background Information

The Nazca culture originated in the well-known Paracas culture (1000–200 B.C.), which was renowned for its weavings and mummy bundles (Engel 1966). The center of the Paracas culture was the region between the Pisco, Nazca, and Ica valleys, bounded on the east by the flanks of the Andes and on the west by the Pacific Ocean. Parallel to the sea was an extensive desert strip. The few rivers flowed irregularly, and little water was available for agriculture except during the period from December to March, when it rained in the Andes. Rivers originating in the highlands collected just enough water for cultivation in the valleys below, and generally did not reach the ocean.

In the nineteenth century, the German archaeologist Max Uhle encountered ceramics in German museums that had no specific identification other than "of Peruvian origin." Between 1886 and 1905 he proceeded to excavate sites on the Peruvian coast to which he gave the name "proto-Nazca" (Uhle 1914). Subsequently Gayton and Kroeber (1927) established a time sequence of four phases to mark the cultural development of the Nazca. John Rowe, at the University of California at Berkeley, a later student of Nazca ceramics, delineated two very different phases: the monumental, with a simple decorative style, and

Figure 8. Erythroxylon coca. (*After Plowman 1981: 198*)

the prolific, which was more complex (Rowe 1960). L. E. Dawson further delineated nine phases for Nazca ceramics based on stratigraphic and typological studies (Pezzia 1972).

Nazca culture is known for its aqueducts, cemeteries, and diverse material remains, and has been widely publicized for the so-called Nazca lines, which are discussed later in this chapter. The complex Nazca system of aqueducts and covered canals, many of which are still in use today by Peruvian farmers, testifies to the organization necessary to obtain the maximum benefit from water in places where high temperatures and the sandy quality of the soil caused water loss. With these irrigation works, the Nazca conserved precious water by channeling every drop to the cultivated fields (Mejia 1949).

To understand the Nazca world view, beliefs, and values, as earlier scholars have reminded us (Yacovleff 1932; Muelle 1937), we must understand the iconography of Nazca ceramics. The iconography reflects a complex world, full of magico-religious ideas, expressed by means of a combination of simple and known elements—birds, men, plants, and fish—mixed with others of symbolic content—trophy heads, plumes, and various appendages. One well-known being combining human and magical attributes has variously been called the "mythological masked being" (fig. 10; see Roark 1965), the "degenerated demon head" (Tello 1915), the "occulated being" (Rowe 1961), and a personage directly related to the "flying god of Paracas" (fig. 11; see Kaufmann 1976). This being is characterized not only by the special position of its body, but also by the extended long hair and arms and legs in movement.

The "flying god of Paracas" is also found in many famous embroidered cloths. It is presented as a disguised or masked personage with a war club and varied magical abilities, with trophy heads and multicolored vestments. This god's prominence in hundreds of years of Nazca art reflects the transmission through generations of the power element that directed the life and activities of man. These fantastic beings, in fact, most probably were depictions of regional religious/political leaders who assumed control over aspects of daily life and the severe ecological limitations of their communities.

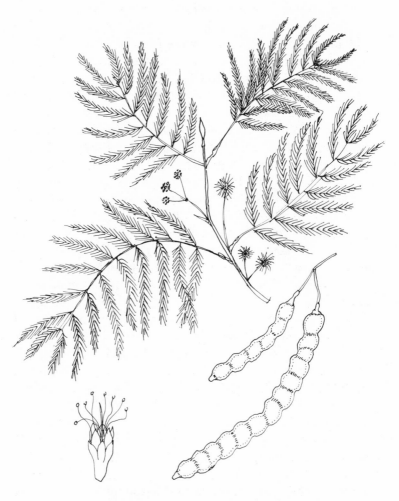

Figure 9. Anadenanthera peregrina. (*After Stafford 1977: 284*)

In the pages to follow, I examine Nazca ceramics in detail, in the light of a growing literature that focuses on the role of plant hallucinogens in the art of non-Western peoples. It is first necessary, however, to examine the hallucinogenic plants present in the Nazca environment.

Students of ancient South American prehistory acknowledge the rich natural laboratory of plant hallucinogens available in Peru (Cooper 1949). Coast, highlands, and rain forest abound in a pharmacopoeia of plants known to alter normal waking consciousness, and the south coast of Peru is no exception. The coca plant (*Erythroxylon coca*), a stimulant, has been documented in the central coastal site of Huaca Prieto from as early as 2500 B.C. It is native to the eastern slopes of the Andes, and free trade between the south coast and the Ayacucho highlands (due east of the Nazca valley) has been documented for a number of economic plants (Ferryere 1979, personal communication). Towle (1961) cites the presence of *Trichocereus pachanoi*, a cactus known for its active ingredient, mescaline, on the southern coast of Peru. Schultes (1967) has written of *cimora*, a cactus drink comprising five different mind-altering cacti, used in witchcraft and healing activities on the north coast of Peru and easily accessible to southern coastal areas. Additionally, Datura plants are still widely used in coastal, highland, and rain forest regions. The *wilka* snuff, *Anadenanthera peregrina*, a major drug plant of the Ayacucho region, was also easily accessible to the ancient Nazca and, later, to the Inca (Altschul 1971).

Wasson has documented that Espingo seeds from the coastal lowlands are sometimes an ingredient in chicha (maize beer): chroniclers said it made people go crazy. Joseph de Arriaga wrote that this dry fruit with round kernels was used as an offering in the *huacas*, or sacred shrines, in the lowlands from Chancay southward (Wasson 1972).

Nazca Art and Plant Hallucinogen Representation

Dr. Cabieses, Director of the Museum of Health Sciences in Lima, has assembled an interesting collection of Nazca ceramics that feature representations of San Pedro and other species of

Figure 10. Nazca mythological masked beings.

cactus. In an unpublished manuscript, he shows that the cross section of a San Pedro cactus, with its peculiar central circular marking, is identical to a star-like representation very commonly used in Nazca art. He also has data showing that the flowering buds of cacti are commonly found in Nazca art. Another stylized motif of graceful, curling lines amply represented the Nazca ceramics suggests to Cabieses the *Datura floripondio*. Other psychoactive plants, however, such as coca or *wilka*, are not represented in Nazca art, despite our knowledge of their general use in coastal and highland pre-Columbian Peru (see Altschul 1972).

The drug plants mentioned earlier, while available in the Nazca region or accessible to this society by means of trade, have not actually been documented in archaeological excavations in this region, except for coca. We do know, of course, that such plants were part of the total plant inventory. I have argued elsewhere (1976) that few pre-Columbian peoples have represented drug plants per se in their art. Such plants were generally used as vehicles to contact more-than-human realms with the intention of dominating the forces of nature, and it is to art related to such use of plants that we must turn to show that, indeed, drug plants were actively used among the Nazca.

Nazca Ceramic Art

The Nazca left behind a rich tradition of ceramics, famous for their aesthetic and technical quality. Such ceramics have been subject to much scrutiny in studies such as those by Blasco and Ramos (1974), Della Santa (1962), Gayton and Kroeber (1927), Lehman (1924), Means (1917), Proulx (1968), Rowe (1960), Schlesier (1959), Seler (1923), Yacovleff (1932), and Zuidema (1971). With my colleague, Dr. Mercedes Cardenas, I examined over 750 ceramic pieces, both in exhibition and in storage, at the National Museum of Anthropology and Archaeology in Lima, the Lima Museum of Art, and the Riva Aguero Institute of the Catholic University in Lima. Many of the arguments that follow are based on these observations.

Roark (1965) wrote a doctoral dissertation on the changes

Figure 11.   The flying god of Paracas.

in Nazca art from the monumental era to the prolific epoch, two
late periods originally delineated by Rowe. His interpretation,
however, does not deal with the subject of religion. As many
anthropologists interested in art have pointed out, in traditional
societies the secularization of art is a rare phenomenon. Certainly, we can conclude that Nazca ceramic traditions are closely
and significantly linked to spiritual concerns. Although Roark's
careful analysis of art style in the formal elements of Nazca
pottery in phases 5 and 6 is a great contribution, some elements
of his analysis can be reexamined from the perspective of plant
hallucinogen use and thematic insight into shamanic beliefs.

A major theme in Nazca art of the monumental and prolific
periods is the "masked mythical being" (see fig. 10), a more or
less human figure, holding a war club and trophy head or heads,
wearing a series of elaborate ornaments, and with a mouth mask.
The theme is found in more than 25 percent of the sample examined by Roark, and it is a prevalent theme in the samples at

Figure 12. Nazca "signifier" motif. (After Roark 1965: fig. 36)

the National Museum of Anthropology and Archaeology in Lima as well. As artistic conventions evolve over time, the anatomical details become "less human" (Roark 1965: 17), and there is a focus on an enormous head and ornaments, with the body and feet relegated to lesser importance. Roark uses the term *signifier* to refer to a complex component of one design theme (see fig. 12). It is a long, flowing streamer appended to the side of the head and composed of a series of bands with elaborate borders. In the Museum of Art in Lima, the signifier is referred to as a worm (*gusano*). Within the signifier, we find trophy heads, darts, fish, or other elements, including wings, an occasional plant, tails, cat face, or serpents. To Roark, different variants of the signifier appear to distinguish slightly different manifestations or aspects of the masked mythical being. Some of the most frequently depicted animal features include those of the fox, feline, bird, and killer whale.

I argue that these varied masked mythical beings represent

powerful shamanic leaders. The animal aspects appended to their signifiers represent their animal or fish familiars, over which they have dominion by means of plant hallucinogen ingestion. Interestingly, in Nazca art, one must argue that the aggregation of various elements within a signifier indicates metaphorically the totality of power of a given religious/political leader. As discussed in chapter 7, below, with regard to the Mochica in northern Peru, we find that the belief in the existence of a spiritual hierarchy in the world of nature is basic to the concept of shamanism. Animals and fish are ranged in order, according to their particular power attributes. Parallel to this hierarchy is another found among men, who differ in their abilities to control and dominate the world of flesh and spirit. The role of plant hallucinogens within this parallel hierarchy allows men to pass over to the world of the spirit and gain some control, or transform themselves into the power objects they desire (see Pitt-Rivers 1970). Further, the hierarchy in the world of animals is by no means based on brute force or size. A small and insignificant creature like the worm may be lauded and admired for its fertility functions, as well as for its communication with the nether worlds below. Its ability to transform itself into a glorious butterfly may be likened metaphorically to the death and resurrection motif also commonly found in drug-using cultures.

Another major theme in Nazca art is that of combat. From the sleeves of the masked mythical being we find the right hand invariably holding a war club and the left hand holding a trophy head. The symbolism of left-right and good-evil, a perennial magico-religious theme, has been pointed out by Furst in his treatment of western Mexican figurines and their shamanic implication (1965). The war club often has bloody spots on it, and Roark (1965) points out that this is the only design element not outlined in Nazca pottery. It flows, while everything else is frozen. The war club is identical to a digging stick held by harvesters and farmers in other ceramic designs. As pointed out above, the function of the shamanic leader in traditional societies is multifaceted—there seems to be some relationship between the shaman's role as defender of the group against evil sorcerers, by means of powers available to him through his hallucinogenic plants, and the fecundity of the earth, ensured by the blood of the enemy. Evil is thus combated, the enemy's head is taken, and the crops are harvested without problem. Additionally, in numerous motifs not only of masked mythical beings, but in what Roark has called sub-major and minor themes in the pottery, we find the breechcloth of the powerful figure painted to depict a trophy head. This is yet another indication of the relationship of the warrior elements, the sexual function (not only of the individual, but of the earth), and the powerful leader.

A major feature accompanying the masked mythical being is the dart or thorn (also called a *chonta* in Spanish). It plays a major role in hallucinogen-linked shamanic healing activities, because one of the major attributes of the shaman is his role as a medicine man or healer. As medical anthropological studies have shown, one of the primary healing motifs in cross-cultural studies deals with a witch's intrusion of a foreign object into his enemy's body; this must be removed, generally by sucking or other magical means, if the patient is to recover. The portrayal of chontas or thorns on the Nazca signifiers indicates yet another emblem of shamanic power. Just as he is able to cause these thorns to enter the body of his enemy to kill him, so, too, can the shaman extract such thorns from his clients to enable them to survive magical illnesses introduced by their enemies.

The "horrible bird" motif, another theme of interest, was discussed by Yacovleff (1932) in terms of power symbols. Nazca pottery, as well as that of other pre-Columbian peoples, shows many bird markings or avian indicators which may represent a mystical identification with birds. Avians are respected and sought-after animal familiars, owing to their extraordinary ability to see their prey from great distances. As hunters, their powers are unique in the animal kingdom. Representations of the hummingbird or *colimbri* indicate an intimacy with the sucking functions of this small creature. The metaphoric element here may be along the lines of "just as the hummingbird sucks at the nectar of flowers, so, too, does the healer suck out the evil thorn introduced there by an evil witch" (see Sharon and Donnan 1974).

Additionally, the representation of the tail as part of the signifier may also refer to the importance of the aerial voyage, which Eliade (1958) has argued represents a shamanic transcendance of the human state. Indeed, the element of flying is omnipresent as a theme in Nazca ceramics. With regard to the phenomenon of relationships between flying and plant-drugs, I have argued that the out-of-body experience, which can be induced by plant hallucinogens or experienced spontaneously, is amply recorded in the psychiatric literature. It can be linked to the experience of flying or to the avian familiar. Shamans commonly report out-of-body experiences in which they leave their physical bodies and assume the shape of familiar(s) to inflict harm to their enemies or to divine the future. In some Nazca pottery, we find trophy heads linked to the wing motif, which may indicate that the end result of the flight is that the enemy is vanquished.

Another motif of interest is that of the killer whale being. Angular jaws and blood are associated with this familiar. In some specimens, knives are appended to the head of a masked mythical being (Roark 1965). The shamanic relationship with the sea also indicates dominion over this force of nature, as well as association with marine plants and other forms of marine life. In Nazca phase 6, there is an interesting feature not explained by Roark, which may be linked to drug ingestion. This is the great enlargement of the head and mouth mask area, without trophy heads or other animal details. One important feature of drug-related shamanism is the role of the breath used to blow tobacco smoke over the head and body of a sick individual or as a protective fumigant against evil spirits. It is not clear to what extent tobacco was utilized in Nazca religion, but in other coastal areas, tobacco plays an important part in modern drug rituals.

Roark argues that there is no portraitism for the Nazca such as that found among the Mochica in the north coast (see chapter 7, below), While the latter portray physical features in detail, the former depict the shamanic leader in all his glory with non-expressive and highly stylized faces, with his physical and spiritual powers indicated by the number and types of animal familiars appended to the signifier.

A greater variety of human figures, however, is found in Nazca phase 6, including harvesters, warriors, farmers, and hunters. Trophy heads are also frequently present, and cacti are a minor theme. In Roark's terminology, mythical-being figures are in great array. Roark sees a change from religion to warfare as a theme, but I disagree. Rather, I suggest, we are viewing an intensification of the importance of the shamanic function. The increased frequency of trophy heads is interesting to examine in this context. I would argue that, while militarism seems to be on the increase, it is not clear whether it is in the form of actual combat or of spiritual warfare. Roark's interpretation is that militarism is on the increase.

While the cult of the mummified or reduced head was very widespread in the American continents (Blasco and Ramos 1974), Lanning (1967) has argued that such trophy heads are late to occur in Peruvian culture. On the south coast, however, the theme appears in Paracas weavings. Anthropomorphic figures have their clothes adorned with heads and also carry them in their hands. Feline and other shamanic elements are usually associated with such heads. Generally, the heads have unkempt hair, which indicates boastfulness over the enemy's defeat in battle. The practice of taking heads as trophies was continued until the Inca period, when it took on a religious character, as punishment and as an offering. Heads were prepared with a cord inserted in the forehead, enabling easy movement from one place to another. The heads may have been exhibited high on a pole. The lips were sewn with a cactus spine needle; some lips were cut just before the head was buried. Trophy heads are found in south coast tombs as well as in necropolis settings, along with decapitated cadavers. Scholars are not sure whether these were voluntary sacrifices or war captives. Nor is it clear whether this practice is limited to one valley or covers tombs of all periods, since so few data are available. Few heads of women are found; those few may indicate punishment for drug-related sorcery, an activity currently found in Peru among mature women as well as among men. Many shamanic elements connected with trophy heads have been pointed out earlier.

The Nazca "Lines"

To the anthropologist interested in the problems of interpreting archaeological remains, particularly the belief systems

and mythologies of now-extinct peoples, the massive earthworks of the New World present a fascinating problem. Mounds
containing burials, as well as massive symbolic earth formations
that are difficult to interpret, can be found in the Nazca region.

In this section, I will argue that shamanistic, plant-hallu-
cinogen-induced, out-of-body experiences—"aerial voyages"—
were the inspiration for the massive earthworks of the prehistoric Nazca. Their purpose was to make certain cosmological
messages known, not only to supernatural forces, but to members of the community as well as to other shamans in conflict
with the social group. To argue this point, I will evaluate the
archaeological record with regard to available data; synthesize
available clinical studies concerning hallucinogen ingestion in
patient and experimental populations; document the out-of-body
experiences associated with such states; and analyze the cogent
characteristics of shamanism pertinent to this theme. To begin
the discussion, I shall briefly summarize our knowledge of the
so-called Nazca lines, or earthworks.

THE EARTHWORKS   Near the hills of the Rio Grande, high in
the elevated desert plains of coastal Peru, we find a vast network
of thousands of straight lines and large dirt drawings on the
ground. Dating to the early Nazca period, about A.D. 1000, these
figures are always found near a large enclosure or a wide road.
Several hundred such earthworks have been recorded by scholars (Kosok 1947; Kosok and Reiche 1949; Reiche 1949). The lines
were made by removing from the path the small stones that
covered the desert and placing them along the sides of the path,
where they form slightly elevated ridges (Reiche 1949: 207–8).
Since virtually no rain falls in this area of the world, preservation
has been fairly continuous. The paths never cross; each figure
is completed close to its beginning. Forms that are discernible
include flying birds, insects, felines, killer whales, fish, spiral
forms (possible coiled snakes), snake-birds, flying pelicans, and
a large plant form. All the earthwork motifs also occur on the
weavings and ceramics of the region. Some earthwork lines are
over 1,700 meters long, while others extend over two and a half
kilometers.

Kosok, an archaeologist, has suggested that they are probably sacred objects made for priests to walk on during festive occasions (1949: 212). Reiche, an astronomer and mathematician, suggests a variety of astronomical significances for lines, which she documents as solstice and equinoctial points upon the horizon (1949: 45). Some scholars have explained them as totem-like symbols which belong to various prehistoric kin groupings. Kubler (1962) acknowledges that the function of the large curved figures of plants and animals is unknown, but suggests that their style is close to early Nazca drawings and speculates that the images are symbolic of constellations. He sees an artistic significance in the lines:

> It is perhaps unexpected, but it is not improper to call these lines, bands, and effigies a kind of architecture. They are clearly monumental, serving as an immovable reminder that here an important activity once occurred. They inscribe a human meaning upon the hostile wastes of nature in a graphic record of a forgotten but one important ritual. They are an architecture of two-dimensional space, consecrated to human actions rather than to shelter and recording a correspondence between the earth and the universe. They are an architecture of diagram and relation, with the substance reduced to a minimum. (1962: 286)

It is interesting to note that most analyses of these earth-works were made only after 1944, when aerial photography could be employed to map them. Kosok (Kosok 1947; Kosok and Reiche 1949) compares them to the animal mounds of the northern United States, just as Coe has seen resemblances among Olmec mounds and Adena/Hopewell and Nazca earthworks (1971). Another scholar, Isbell (1978), has argued that the energy investment necessary to create the ground drawing efforts in the Nazca area represent an effort comparable to that which created the monumental adobe structures of the Mochica to the north.

OUT-OF-BODY EXPERIENCES The evidence for plant hallucin-ogen use in Peru has been discussed. I would like to turn my attention to a commonly reported subjective effect of plant hal-lucinogen use, namely the "out-of-body experience." Green has labeled this experience the "ecosomatic effect," defined as "objects of perception organized in such a way that the observer sees himself to be observing them from a point of view not coincident with his physical body" (1968: 111). Throughout much of the nonscientific literature, this subjective state has been reported frequently to occur spontaneously without any chemical intervention. Nonetheless, such experiences are also a common feature of the hallucinogenic experience (Hofmann 1959; Masters and Houston 1966; Tart 1971); they are often referred to as a "depersonalization effect" (see Ludwig 1969: 14). Ludwig has described a wide array of distortions in body image that occur in all altered states of consciousness as a schism between body and mind, or a dissolution of boundaries between the self and the other, the world, or the universe. Another state, which Green titles the "asomatic state," is an ecosomatic state in which the subject is temporarily unaware of being associated with *any* body or spatial entity. Barber, in summarizing the clinical studies of LSD and other psychoactive drugs up to 1970, wrote of the changes in body image as well. Practically all subjects state that their body "feels strange or funny. More bizarre feelings are registered at higher drug doses, such as a body melting into the background or floating in space" (1970: 22).

Dr. Roland Atkinson, a former colleague of mine at the California College of Medicine, University of California, Irvine, was involved in a research project examining the effect of nitrous oxide on man. He summarizes the literature on out-of-body experiences (n.d.) and uses the term *autoscopy*, a general term meaning the perception, usually visual, of one's own physical body in objective space. He uses the term *external autoscopy* for the perception in an out-of-body experience of one's own body in objective space. Atkinson argues that a subject may respond to heightened awareness as pleasant or instructive, particularly if he seeks it out through training and repeated efforts, including using hallucinogenic drugs. On a continuum of effects, the out-of-body experience includes those in which the subject sees his physical body in objective space but experiences no body-like container that encompasses the external locus of the subject's awareness. The term *self* is more appropriate than *body* in this context. Reports of such experiences usually emphasize the otherworldly, mystical, and paranormal nature of perception. This type of experience tends to be associated with profound, drug-induced, altered states of consciousness.

Atkinson's interests have been in the neurological and psychiatric dimensions involved in the production of such states, a topic outside the scope of this book. However, this discussion should illustrate the relationship between drug induction and the subjective effects of the out-of-body experience, which I would like to link to the shamanistic ingestion of plant hallucinogens among the ancient Nazca. As Eliade has argued, ecosomatic experiences, drug-induced and otherwise, have been reported with shamanistic religion. He has commented as follows on the meaning of these aerial voyages:

> Siberian, Eskimo and North American shamans fly. All over the world, the same magical power is credited to sorcerers and medicine men. . . . All this makes us think of the ornithomorphic symbolism of the Siberian shamans' costumes. . . . According to many traditions, the power of flight extended to all men in the mythical age; all could reach heaven whether on wings of a fabulous bird or on the clouds. . . . We should make it clear, however, that here such powers often take on a purely spiritual character; flight expresses only intelligence, understanding of secret things or metaphysical truths. . . . Magical flight is the expression of both the soul's autonomy and of ecstasy. The myth of the soul contains in embryo a whole metaphysic of man's spiritual autonomy and freedom. . . . The point of primary importance here is the mythology and the rites of magical flight peculiar to shamans and sorcerers confirm and proclaim their transcendence in respect to the human condition; by flying into the air, in bird form or in their normal human shape, shamans proclaim the degeneration of humanity. (1958: 480–81)

DISCUSSION   To link the phenomenon of drug-induced shamanistic out-of-body experiences with the image mounds and earthworks of the Nazca requires a discussion of features of shamanism relevant to the data presented earlier on Nazca ceramic art. I would particularly like to examine the role of the shaman as the psychopomp, the spiritual guardian of a community, who is obliged to confront and combat his group's adversaries. His major activities include healing disease and neutralizing misfortunes that have befallen members of the community through the machinations of enemies. Shamans are famous for their ability to transform themselves into powerful animal figures—animal familiars or *naguals,* in Pitt-Rivers's terminology—whom they send to do their bidding, to rectify evil or redress the harm caused their clients. These familiars are generally chosen because of some characteristics which, through sympathetic magic, are believed controllable by the shaman. In my opinion, the effigies of animals found throughout the New World massive earthworks represent these shamanic familiars. I would argue that the drug-using shaman, with spirit familiars on call to serve him, has a subjective experience which includes the sensation of flying. My point is quite simple: one need not literally fly in the air to experience flight. Thus the Nazca earthworks, difficult for the Westerner to conceptualize visually without an airplane voyage or aerial photograph, are perhaps more simply explicable as the projection by the shaman of the animal or totem familiar from the heights of ecstasy through which he soars.

Some of the earthworks have geometric rather than animal shapes, and these may be linked to another common LSD-like effect. Visionary patterns frequently reported by drug users are the kaleidoscopic geometric forms that Barber (1970) has argued may represent a change in retinal structure. In fact, it has been hypothesized (Marshall 1937; Kluver 1942) that entoptic phenomena—visual phenomena that have their seat within the eye, such as small specks, spots, or other objects drifting across the field of vision with movements of the eyes and of the cones and rods in our eyeballs—are perceived under the effects of the drug. Further studies are needed to verify the hypothesis that drugs lower the threshold for the perception of entoptic phenomena (Barber 1970: 32–33).

Given the arguments for the militant nature of the shaman,

protecting his community against the evil doings of others as well as serving as intermediary with the supernatural, I view such monumental earthworks as constructed to warn rival shamans of the powers that were controlled by the psychopomp of a given area, to reaffirm supernatural contact, and to maintain social solidarity. The enormous expenditures of labor and cooperation needed to construct such earthworks, extending perhaps from generation to generation, reaffirmed the bonds that link men together. Such ties of cooperation maintain intragroup harmony and are important in small-scale societies. Finally, as we have seen, the symbolic forms of the image mounds consisted of elements of ritualized belief already present in the plastic arts of the Nazca.

Conclusion

While the evidence must remain circumstantial that the Nazca used plant hallucinogens in their religious rituals, we know that plant hallucinogens were present in southern Peru and available for their use. Representations of plant drugs in Nazca art are limited to various cactus species and, possible, Datura plants. Nazca ceramic motifs and the over-arching shamanic belief system parallel those of other drug-using New World cultures where we have independent verification of plant hallucinogenic drug use from ethnohistorical sources. The possible use of plant hallucinogens among these ancient peoples has been examined to suggest that the Nazca leader, within the framework of power over his fellow man and over nature, may have imbibed such psychoactive plants to enable him to function in accordance with the values and goals of his culture.

Chapter 6

The New Guinea Highlanders

The Kuma and Kaimbi are unique among the world's people in the way they have incorporated drug plants into daily life. Elsewhere hallucinogens are used in religious and magical ritual, but these tribal groups, located in the highland region of New Guinea, employ several hallucinogenic mushrooms in relatively mundane, secular ways. Their hallucinogen use is connected by most scholars with the resolution of intragroup tension and conflict.

Living in the Wahgi Valley of the Western New Guinea highlands, the two tribes are very much like other highland peoples whose culture depends upon horticultural activities, in this case, raising sweet potatoes, bananas, maize, beans, and sugarcane. Pigs also play an important role in their culture. A very secular, sensate people, as anthropologist Marie Reay has called them (1959), the Kuma lack any complex belief systems connected to the preternatural that have to do with mushrooms. Reay has characterized Kuma culture in general as hedonistic, involved in a series of mundane activities oriented toward self-aggrandizement and display, control of women, and accumulation of pig wealth. Values such as pursuit of one's reputation and triumph over others, antagonism between men and women, opposition between youth and age, and division of people into

classes of kinsmen and strangers embrace the major foci of Kuma/
Kaimbi society. Such is the setting for their quite distinctive use
of hallucinogenic fungi. The ingestion of such plants is just one
means among others of achieving secular cultural goals.

The Mushrooms

In 1947, an anthropologist who worked in the Mt. Hagen
highland region of New Guinea, A. L. Gitlow, wrote about the
use of a wild mushroom, locally called *nonda*, which excited
tribesmen to a combative frenzy. Gitlow quotes Father Ross, the
missionary who worked among these people in 1934, as follows:
"The wild mushroom called nonda makes the user temporarily
insane. He flies into a fit of frenzy. Death was known to have
resulted from its use at times. The plant was taken before going
out to kill another native or in times of great excitement, anger
or sorrow" (cited in Heim and Wasson 1958, 1965).

Today the highlanders use the term *nonda* generically to
describe all mushrooms. In this Western highland region of New
Guinea, the Kuma use the Pandanus, Boletus, and Psilocybe
mushrooms, which cause double vision, cold shivers, hallucinations, and loss of speech. Women, especially, report hallucinations while under the influence of the fungi.

In the anthropological literature, until recently, few of the
mushrooms used by the Kuma were identified properly. Too
often, field workers tumbled upon them serendipitously, lacking
proper techniques to dry or store the plants until they could be
shipped to botanical laboratories for identification. Both Reay
(1960) and Nelson (1970) lost samples for this reason. A team of
investigators who have added greatly to our knowledge of highland New Guinea mushrooms were the French mycologist Roger
Heim and the amateur mycologist Gordon Wasson. They visited
New Guinea for a few weeks in 1961 in an attempt to identify
and collect the *nonda* mushroom (Heim and Wasson 1965). Although the Kuma eat the mushroom all year long, it is only in
the dry season that people manifest signs of what has commonly
been called "the mushroom madness" (Reay 1960).

The Kuma identify four distinctive mushrooms in the highlands: a white fungus with a yellow stem, a small reddish one with a white stem, an orange-colored fungus, and a fourth that is thick-stemmed and orange, with the middle section of the stem purple when fresh. All four grow on dead logs (Reay 1960). Prior to 1965, when chemical identification showed that the Boletus mushrooms, at least, contained traces of indolic LSD-like substances, and a new species of Psilocybe was identified, most scholars advanced educated guesses as to the identity of these mushrooms. Schultes, the renowned botanist, argued that several species of Russula might have been responsible for the psychoactive effects (see also Heim 1963).

Mushroom Madness

The Kuma are one of the best-studied peoples who exhibit symptoms of the "mushroom madness." We have a reasonable amount of information on how the mushrooms affect them, both from accounts of anthropologists and from the letters of Europeans who lived in their valley and were frequently struck—and quite frightened—by the "wild men of the Wahgi." A missionary couple, Mr. and Mrs. Phillips, described an occasion upon which six young men under the influence of mushrooms rushed about chasing people and threatening them with spears. The Phillipses wrote that the mushroom madness could be traced to the eating of what they thought were toadstools, or poisonous mushrooms. They described the drug as blurring the eyes and making people deaf and crazy, chasing up and down the mountain. Limitless in energy, both men and women were affected. The women were seen to dance, whistle, and sing. They giggled, laughed, and let out loud yells. They were affected with a type of drunkenness that lasted for a couple of days (Heim and Wasson 1965). Other descriptions are similar, featuring brandishing of spears by men, from which people ran for their lives. Generally, however, people suffered no more than an occasional wound from a badly aimed arrow.

We can summarize what is known of Kuma mushroom madness. When women partake, they become delirious and irresponsible, begin to dance and sing, and have their husbands or sons decorate them in their best feathers. They are even given weapons to hold. At this time, married women are permitted to dance in formation in the way that men and unmarried girls do. When the women return to their houses, they boast of real or imaginary sexual adventures. When a woman feels that an attack is forthcoming, she will plunge into a nearby river if she does not want to exhibit herself. Although mushrooms are eaten in all seasons of the year by young and old, men and women, and are mixed with other vegetables, the Kuma attribute this madness to the mushrooms, although it occurs only in the dry season. No ritual preparation accompanies the madness (Reay 1960).

Men under the effects of the plant behave differently. They put on all kinds of ornaments, take up their weapons, and run about terrorizing everyone in sight. Attacking their clansmen and families, they often stray to other communities to frighten distant relatives. They are described as tense and excited—they shiver in the extremities of their fingers, they report seeing double, and they seem to suffer from aphasia.

Although minor injuries have been reported, the mushroom madness rarely, if ever, leads to serious wounds and never to death. Heim (Heim and Wasson 1965) found this fact noteworthy, since elsewhere maniacs do find their mark on occasion. In fact, relatives are attacked only when spectators are present, at which time the attacker can be held back if necessary. Interestingly enough, when several men are afflicted with the madness, they tend not to pay attention to one another, but only to those unaffected (Reay 1959). Heim and Wasson (1965) describe the social excitement connected with teasing individuals in this state. Women and boys, in search of an exciting diversion, deliberately encourage men to be aggressive. For those men who are the chief protagonists in this social drama, it is a departure from normal activity which they are able to joke about at a later date. People who are affected by the mushrooms are not stigmatized in any way, nor do they achieve any kind of prestige as the result of this temporary aberration. Rather, the Kuma believe that the people involved are not responsible for their activities.

In 1954, Reay found 30 persons out of 313 tribesmen, or

some 10 percent of her sample, seized by the madness (1960). Another 8 had in the past been affected, but on this particular occasion, they escaped the effects of the plant. Reay's informants claimed that the mushroom madness seemed to run in families: a person was likely to be subject to the madness if either of his parents was afflicted. Nonetheless, several of the affected individuals observed by Reay did not have any hereditary predisposition. It is interesting that children are never subject to mushroom madness. Heim and Wasson (1965) concluded that social customs were responsible for the madness; the custom provided a social catharsis for members of Kuma society. Another interpretation of those investigators was that the transvestite behavior of women symbolized their alteration of traditional low status, in the form of a rite of rebellion, much like Sadie Hawkins Day.

There is general agreement in the Wahgi Valley that the feats of endurance performed by wild men far exceed their normal physical activity. Rushing up and down mountain trails, these individuals shake their weapons about and shout as loud as they can. Similar feats, of course, have been reported for Siberian Koryak and Chukchee, who used the *Amanita muscaria* mushrooms discussed in chapter 3.

Nelson (1970), who worked among the Kaimbi-speaking peoples in the Nebilyer Valley and on the southern slopes of the Kubor Mountains, has observed the mushroom madness in more recent times. Living in the same geographical area as the Kuma, and sharing basic social patterns, the Kaimbi informants reported peak periods of mushroom madness shortly after the end of the wet season, in late May and early June. According to folk beliefs the madness results from the ingestion of any of several species of mushrooms; the type of madness depends upon the species eaten. Nelson reported that among the Kaimbi, people mentioned such symptoms as shaking fits, tremors, multiple vision, jumping up and down on one foot, and "amok" behavior. During this last condition, the hallucinating individual picked up an axe or spear and ran through inhabited areas attempting attacks upon whomever he encountered. Nelson's report is similar in many respects to Reay's (1959, 1960) on the

Kuma, although the Kaimbi do not express what Reay has labeled "patterned lewdness' in association with mushroom use, nor do they claim any hereditary determination for such states. Certainly, mild hallucinogens do affect people quite diversely and individual psychological factors are important to consider. Nelson, like Reay, has examined aspects of mushroom madness in terms of the contribution of cultural factors in the etiology of the condition. Both the Kuma and Kaimbi define the madness as temporary insanity. Among the Kaimbi, too, Nelson found no instance of persons who were seriously wounded or killed by a mushroom-crazed individual. Nelson has argued that there are socially defined limits to overt behavioral patterns associated with mushroom madness.

Although running-amok behavior may have some cathartic value, and may be what anthropologists like to consider a "ritual of rebellion," we cannot, of course, eliminate the possibility that there is some chemical effect of the mushroom which is responsible for the madness. Certainly, traces of indolic substances in the *Boletus* would substantiate this hypothesis, and in fact, in 1967, Heim identified a new species of Psilocybe, called *Psilocybe kumaenorum*, similar to the Mexican variety, which gives conclusive evidence for the actual presence of alkaloids. According to Nelson (1970) most of the New Guineans are conversant with the more than fifty varieties of fungi in their environment. It is improbable that people with such extensive knowledge of the plant would have been deluded about the effects of only a few varieties, as originally postulated by Heim and Wasson (1965) before chemical analysis of the Russula species showed small amounts of indolic substances present. As T. McGuire postulates in analyzing the mushroom use of the ancient Maya (1982), varying demands for different species of the genera Psilocybe, Stropharia, Conocybe, and Panaeolus may have been related to Mayan theological needs. In that ancient society, the alteration of normal waking consciousness may have been varied to utilize the specific perceptual effects caused by different species. McGuire argues that organized exchange of mushrooms by the Maya may have been intended to meet the supplies and demands of personal preferences, specific purposes, and seasonal and regional

Figure 13.   Boletus mushroom, New Guinea. (After Schultes and Hofmann 1973: 36)

availability. Different physical, emotional, and psychopharaco-
logic responses can be obtained from different plants. Emboden,
too, has argued that a single plant may have multiphasic effects
because of its chemistry or according to its dosage (1979: 162).

The "accidental" affliction with the madness that has been
reported with some frequency among the Kaimbi peoples is also
interesting to examine in light of the arguments about "cultural
drama" that were originally posed by Reay, Heim, and Wasson.
Despite the emphasis that these authors originally placed upon
the cathartic and pleasurable aspects of violent and delusional
behavior among the Kuma, the Kaimbi data, in contrast, point
out the unanimous feeling reported by tribesmen concerning
the "bad trip" effects of the mushrooms (Nelson 1970). Native
Kaimbi reports of drug-induced altered states of consciousness
have included fear of hallucination, fear of hurting someone,
fear of having to be subdued by one's kinsmen, or terrible fright
at the thought of spending the night alone in the bush. Some
people, nonetheless, purposely eat the mushrooms; although
they are aware of what will happen, they like the juice of the
plant and probably the side effects. Although the Kuma and
Kaimbi share certain cultural similarities, there are differences
between them. The mushroom madness, as Nelson pointed out,
transcends the differences.

Similar forms of running-amok behavior have been described by various anthropologists for this area of the world.
Reay (1960) summarizes running amok as a kind of institutionalized deviance that permits individuals at certain times of stress
to channel antisocial sentiments into a limited range of activities.
Although open aggression toward kinsmen is strongly disap-
proved, running-amok behavior permits such social expression
without penalty or stigma. Reay further has argued that the
mushroom madness among the Kuma seems to be an institutionalized form of tendencies that are normally forbidden expression: women may have a real nostalgia for their years of courtship
and the men for real aggression against members of their own
group. The madness, then, is a periodic expression of behavior
that is considered antisocial during normal times.

Given the fact that the mushrooms can cause mild hallucinatory activity, this is a case where cultural elaboration of a variable chemical effect is related to a particular cultural matrix. Thus, New Guinea mushroom use is characterized by a focus on intragroup drug response when compared to the establishment in other societies of relationships between man and the supernatural. It is interesting to see how small doses of these hallucinogenic substances can lead to aggressive behavior toward one's clansmen and affinal kinsmen, to irresponsible boasting, or to forbidden dances. Reay has argued that the "big men," or sorcerers, who find other cultural channels for the constant expression of aggression, are not affected by eating the fungus.

Chapter 7

The Mochica of Peru

On the north coast of Peru, an ancient civilization, the Mochica, is renowned for its art, especially painted and modeled ceramics. During the summer of 1967, I conducted fieldwork on traditional folk healing in this region, where hallucinogenic plants are an integral part of the treatment of disease (see Dobkin de Rios 1968a, 1968b, 1971, 1973). In extending my analysis from populations currently using plant hallucinogens to prehistoric ones of the same region known only by their archaeological remains, I was surprised at the lack of interest and the superficial assessment made by a variety of scholars concerned with the Mochica, especially in terms of examining the role, if any, that such plant hallucinogens may have played in Mochica religion. Archaeologists and art historians generally have not shown an inclination to deal directly with the effects of psychoactive substances on the belief systems of prehistoric, non-Western societies (see Dobkin de Rios 1974a). This is a pattern one encounters despite the existence of a large scientific literature drawn from the fields of psychiatry, neurology, psychopharmacology, history of religions, mythology, botany, and cultural anthropology.

In this chapter, I will reverse the usual scholarly priorities by considering what I believe to be pivotal in traditional Mochica life—namely, the use of various plant hallucinogens to achieve contact with supernatural realms and to permit individuals to manipulate supernatural forces in order to serve social goals.

In 1967, during my study of the San Pedro cactus use in folk healing (*Trichocereus pachanoi*), I was intrigued by the possible prehistoric roots of plant hallucinogen use. This interest remained dormant until several years later when several publications on Mochica life appeared (Benson 1972; Benson 1974; Sharon and Donnan 1974), which attempted to interpret the large corpus of ceramics left by Mochica craftsmen. Benson (1972), in particular, should be commended for the fine job that she has done in assembling in one place so many of the known materials on the Mochica. However, despite the existence of a literature on modern use of plant hallucinogens on the north coast of Peru (e.g., Friedberg 1960, 1965; Gillen 1947; Sharon 1972a, 1972b), Benson did not fully integrate such materials into her studies of prehistoric art. She only occasionally mentioned the possibility of plant hallucinogen use, or when discussing certain ceramics, she treated "hallucinations" in a disembodied fashion.

In this chapter, I argue that Mochica art, like that of the Nazca, can best be interpreted as an interplay of complex shamanistic notions of good and evil, power and its manipulation and expression, and the magical control over nature by religious hierophants in serving their clients and their community.

Modern Hallucinogen Use in Northern Peru

The Peruvian north coast is a desert, occasionally watered by rivers flowing from east to west. Today, agricultural villages dot the landscape, some of which, like Salas, have become famous throughout all of Peru because they are areas where specialized healers, called *maestros*, treat disease with the use of plant hallucinogens. The most commonly used is the San Pedro cactus, containing 1.29 g of mescaline in a given sample of fresh material. The cactus is cut into small pieces and boiled several hours with additives such as *misha* (*Datura arborea*), *condorillo* (*Lycopodium* sp.), and *hornamo* (unidentified). In addition, to-

Figure 14. Tambos of differing strata of Mochica society; probable San Pedro sessions in each. (After Kutscher 1967: 120)

bacco mixed with water is used as a snuff and drawn into the healer's lungs to enhance a drug's effect.

The major use of San Pedro at present is to treat illness believed to be caused by witchcraft. As with other hallucinogenic plants, San Pedro is used as a revelatory agent to make known the source of bewitchment deemed responsible for illness and misfortune. Healing sessions take place at night in *tambos,* wall-less shelters generally found in fields some distance from houses (see fig. 14). A healer, his assistant, and several patients assemble around a cloth, called a *mesa,* which is laid on the ground. A large number of ritual items, including polished shields and staffs, are set up as defenses against the evil machinations of witches, with other magical elements placed on the mesa. In interviews with healers in 1967, I elicited statements that polished stones are believed to assume the form of persons and animals who attack enemies. During the session, the maestro sings and whistles to invoke spirit forces who will ensure that healing will occur, and also aid in the recognition of the disease. The healers claim that visions from the cactus enable them to learn about the magical illness afflicting their patients (see also Sharon [1972a, 1972b] for documentation of another mesa).

A Recreation of the Mochica World

The pre-Incaic Mochica civilization flourished in the north coastal area of Peru from 100 B.C. until about A.D. 700. The Mochica were a state society with subsistence based on intensive agriculture, including the use of irrigation, and on fishing from one-man canoes made of rushes. These techniques enabled large populations to exploit both maritime and farming areas. According to Gordon R. Willey, "The Mochica built castle-like fortifications over a hundred feet high, out of thousands or millions of adobe bricks. They ran stone and adobe defensive walls for miles across the desert and built great aqueducts of equal length" (personal communication). Mochica society was probably theocratically organized. There was a complex division of labor, with specializations of occupations and crafts. Throughout the ceramic representations, often interpreted as realistic, we see the Mochica warrior, the weaver, the beggar, and the shaman/priest. Mochica society was highly stratified, a pattern reflected in dress, ornament, and temple form. Professions were symbolized by details of dress and ornament, and variations in architecture indicated cult centers.

Some ceramics show surgical and medical practices, while shamanistic sessions very much like those described by myself and others in the literature on present-day regional healing are found in the pottery. Bennett and Bird (1946: 104) have described medicine men performing cures by massaging patients and sucking the affected part of a body to remove a foreign substance, reminiscent of present-day practices. Stylized decorative motifs on Mochica pottery described by the ethnobotanist Friedberg, and interpreted to her by the late Dr. Larco of the Larco Herrera Museum in Lima, depict what seem to be Mochica sorcerers carrying stumps of cacti in their hands. Friedberg suggests that one such representation showed a remarkable likeness to San

Pedro, easily recognized by the lack of thorns (1960: 42). She also describes Mochica pottery showing individuals transformed into animals in association with a thornless cactus. Supernatural forces of a magical nature are represented in the art, including various animals which probably correspond to the nagual, or animal familiar, as well as what Lavallée (1970: 110) has called animal, vegetable, and object demons. Lanning (1967: 122) wrote that Mochica potters portrayed at least 35 different species of birds, 16 of mammals, and 16 of fish, as well as other animals.

Although the Conquest chroniclers' discussions of botanical materials are another source of data, many of these data, unfortunately, are based on vernacular usage and are not always faithful enough for rigorous botanical determination. Cobo (1956), for example, has described San Pedro's use under the name of *achuma*. As long as folk healers did not bring the Devil into their healing rites, Franciscan priests let them maintain some sort of *modus vivendi*, and folk healers were admitted to the Church. Many Roman Catholic beliefs have been syncretized with traditional use of San Pedro cactus.

Mochica Plant Use

Before discussing Mochica religion, it is important to reiterate the evidence of Mochica plant hallucinogen use. As mentioned earlier, various uprooted cacti are represented in the art, including San Pedro. Towle (1961) wrote that Cereus cacti are found frequently in the art of this region. Schultes's references to Cimora (1967, 1972a) from the Peruvian north coast include the cactus *Neoraimondia macrostibas*. Coca played an important economic role in Mochica civilization, as attested in numerous ceramics. Disselhoff (1967: 51) has reproduced a ceramic of a man drinking chicha, the fermented corn drink, with his hand on his coca pouch. Multiple drug use, moreover, was not infrequent, and coca may have been ingested along with other hallucinogenic plants. The effects of mixing such plants remain uncharted by the way (see Schultes 1972b). The possibility of hallucinogenic snuffs must be mentioned, especially since ongoing San Pedro ingestion is found with liquid tobacco snuff. This combination, however, is yet to be documented for the Mochica.

Shamanic Themes in Mochica Art

Prominent in Mochica art is a combative shamanistic ethos, which was reflected in the expansionist military activities of these ancient peoples. I have reported combative elements in shamanistic activity for two distinctive contemporary Peruvian drug-using regions, as has Furst for western Mexico (1965). Despite themes of peace and love reflected in American youth drug use of the late 1960s and early 1970s, we must not ethnocentrically assume that the ethos of one subculture extends to that of another people. Much of nuclear American plant hallucinogen use, in fact, occurs in societies with overriding martial activity, to wit, the Aztec and the Inca. The use of hallucinogenic plants as a means of making the supernatural realm accessible can be concordant with any number of different world views. At any rate, the Americanist commonplace of the last fifty years, reiterated by La Barre (1970b), is that shamanistic beliefs, particularly direct relevation of the supernatural, are dominant motifs of many New World Indian populations.

In Mochica life, shamans probably had an important role as protectors of seafaring activities (see fig. 15), in addition to their duties of healing and of psychopomp as explained by Eliade (1958). A student of San Pedro use observed a healer in Trujillo, Peru, who was called upon by fishermen to bless a forthcoming expedition with the cactus drink (Sharon, personal communication). Amazonian shaman healers often boasted to me of their apprenticeship period when they obtained magical powers over their allies, a long, arduous and often lethal task. When the shaman emerges triumphant, he indeed is believed to be possessed of impressive power. The shaman descending to nether worlds to consult with ancestral spirits is often found in Mochica ceramics (see fig. 22), as is travel to celestial realms, from which the shaman returns with special chants and auguries of future happenings.

Figure 15. The Mochica shaman as protector of seafaring activities. (After Kutscher 1967: 119)

These general comments concerning shamanism are important in my reconstruction of Mochica religion. While we can never hope to plumb the depths of metaphor, analogy, and myth that characterize all traditional religions, I think that we can make a convincing argument to link the effects of plant hallucinogens to Mochica belief systems.

THE SHAMAN AS WARRIOR   As we can see from figure 16, what has been traditionally called the warrior of Mochica culture may also be interpreted as a shaman battling against adversaries. The armor, maces, trophy heads, and various weapons found on the ceramics may be not only the ordinary paraphernalia of war and victory but also shamanistic protection against evil forces. Peruvian gold objects often include war materiel such as maces, which may have alternate magical or symbolic meanings. Many of the ceramics show battle scenes between two individuals, with the figure to the left often subdued by the one on the right. The relationship of left and right to good and evil has been discussed

Figure 16.   The Mochica shamanic battle-combative motif. (After Larco Hoyle 1939: 49)

by Furst (1965: 60) in global shamanistic activities. Hieratic rank-ing relating to shamanistic activity is shown in much Mochica pottery, by use of details of dress and headgear, as well as by step motifs, as are elaborate buildings where religious activity probably took place. The tambo, for example, represented in figure 14, is found both on the Peruvian coast and in the rain forest. In 1967 I observed several drug sessions held in tambos on the coast.

THE SHAMAN AS HEALER   A large number of Mochica pots presented by Benson (1972) illustrate the vital role of the shaman as healer. In many of her illustrations, figures drink from chalice-like cups in public places (although Benson does not link folk healing to many of the scenes portrayed in the pottery). Benson overlooks the significance of the tambo, however. Figure 14 shows an interesting variety of tambos, linked probably to hieratic rank-ing of religious practitioners within this segmented society, from the folk healer in his simple shelter to the powerful priest in a more elegant edifice. It is interesting to note in this context that, owing to the Humboldt current, it rarely rains in the north coast region, so explanations of tambos as protection against the elements are not readily admissible as alternate possibilities.

A point of contention in interpreting Mochica pottery concerns the role of the nude male, often with hair awry, who is led to a stylized tambo, shown under the control of another figure, or else is seated alone (see fig. 17). These nude figures, likened to other such individuals found in art from other areas of Mesoamerica where militaristic conquest characterized social life, are often believed by art historians to be victims of warfare, about to be sacrificed. Although this is a pan-American trait, the figures' nakedness is cited as a sign that the nude male is being humiliated, perhaps prior to his sacrifice. My initial response to such a motif was that the nudity and the presence of a coiled rope around the prisoners' necks might better be viewed as a representation of a severly disordered patient of a folk healer or priest. The latter group may have been administering brews of *Trichocereus pachanoi, Datura arborea,* or other plants to calm hyperactive, maniacal individuals. The clothing and weapons of the nude individuals in figure 17 are tied to the mace of the individual leading them. The special haircut associated with these individuals could have been to represent the mark of the insane; the ravaged faces might have attested to mental illness, then, rather than to the individual's fear of being sacrificed. In this connection, ethnohistorical data from the Aztec indicate that when war prisoners were sent to their death, they were generally given hallucinogenic mushrooms to make them gay and happy before the sacrifice.

After I visited the Mochica archive assembled by Christopher Donnan at the University of California, Los Angeles, I found still another explanation to be possible, drawn from a key motif available in the archive. In one ceramic motif, a figure seated under a tambo structure looks at a large pot which is similar to those used to hold the boiled potions of the San Pedro and other hallucinogenic brews. Around the neck of the pot, a coiled "rope" extends horizontally in the air, becoming a double-headed snake. I argue that the "rope" found throughout Mochica

Figure 17.   Probable defeated Mochica shamanic adversaries, led by victors. (After Kutscher 1950: 179)

pottery, often around the neck of an alleged prisoner, may be a metaphoric abbreviation for the double-headed serpent, pointing to a victorious shaman's animal familiar and its success in subduing the sorcerer's adversary (see fig. 18).

One of the major reasons to suspect that Mochica pottery has religious themes complementing more secular ones has to do with the important role of music and musicians in the incised pots. Individuals are portrayed with special costumes, and instruments and rattles of one type or other are often shown (see fig. 19). The role of music in bridging realms of consciousness made available by hallucinogenic drugs has been analyzed by Katz and myself (Katz and Dobkin de Rios 1971; Dobkin de Rios and Katz 1975). Generally speaking, among drug-using societies music is an important adjunct to hallucinogenic drug use (see also Dobkin de Rios 1973: 178). The vast majority of Mochica pots are of the stirrup type, which can be made to whistle. In the tropical rain forest, I elicited information from drug-using healers that their whistling incantations evoked spirit forces (1972b: 132).

Mochica ceramics are well known in art circles for their erotic themes (see Larco Hoyle 1969), showing individuals in copulatory positions as well as practicing sodomy and bestiality. The presence of sexual themes in the ceramics may indicate more than a merely lusty interest in life, namely a link to shamanistic activity (see fig. 20). There is an interesting relationship between sex and death in Mochica pottery, which may have to do with the expected role of the shaman in ensuring the fertility of the community's women and in dealing with the anxiety generated by the reproductive process in general. Lévi-Strauss (1963) illustrates shamanic interventions in difficult childbirth, giving us a clue to this relationship in the art.

Sexual Themes in Mochica Art

Sexual themes in Mochica art represent a small percentage of the total design repertory (Kauffmann 1978: 21). Bushnell (1965) concludes that 2 percent of Mochica ceramics available for analysis feature well-known sexual themes. Authors such as

Figure 18. The rope motif in Mochica art. (After Sawyer 1966: 51)

Figure 19.   Mochica musicians in pageant, with animal familiars. (*After Benson 1972: 112*)

Figure 20.   Mochica tambo scene, linked with fecundity rituals and shamanistic animal familiars. (*After Benson 1972: 134–35*)

Benson (1972) and Donnan (1976) agree that sexual representations in the art are almost always of a magico-religious character. In 1978, Federico Kauffmann published two volumes in
Spanish and English entitled *Sexual Behavior in Ancient Peru,* in
which he organized information on the sexual art of Peru. Prior
to this publication, Larco Hoyle had published on this topic
(1939) and established a museum in Lima to house his personal
collection. Additionally, Urteaga-Ballon (1968) published a book
that focused on the medical aspects of sexual representations in
Peruvian ceramic art. However, while the contributions of these
authors have been notable in organizing the vast array of information concerning sexual themes in coastal Peruvian ceramics,
none of them has focused on the role plant hallucinogens might
play in influencing these designs. It is important to categorize
sexual themes in the ceramics in terms of their main thematic
components. Linkages to plant drugs, shamanic power, and
population control in a harsh and hostile environment will emerge
from such an approach.

DESCRIPTION OF THE CERAMICS   In addition to a large number
of ceramics of nude figures, both male and female, the art of
coastal Peru shows different coital positions, fellatio, and sodomy. Some nude figures are presented without any genitals.
Ceramics are found with exaggerated phalli (see fig. 21), and
others have been presented with great anatomical attention to
detail. Although the phallus is presented in exaggerated and
personified form, the vulva is rarely presented this way. There
are a series of pottery vessels modeled with erect phalli, which
may have served as drinking vessels. In order to drink any liquid
from the vessel, one had to be very careful, since the neck of
the upper rim is full of holes purposely made and the liquid
leaks and wets the drinker who tries to drink from the top
opening. However, the main cavity of the vessel connects to the
tip of the penis, and if the drinker does not wish to get wet, he
must drink the liquid through the penis.

Many of the ceramics are presented in association with animals and plants or musical instruments, and death motifs are
not unfamiliar. Some of the themes show heterosexual caresses
and precoital activity. Kissing is rarely shown. Copulating

Figure 21. Mochica man with exaggerated phallus.

women lack facial expression. Cunnilingus is not represented nor is masturbation shown with any frequency. Some indication of the fecundity of plants and fish may be found, in association with animals and man. Animated orgies of death-like figures holding drinks in their hands are shown in diverse scenes on walls, ceramics, and terra-cotta sculpture. Childbirth is represented on the pottery.

Some ceramics represent animal copulation with four-footed creatures, 20 percent of the sample being toads. The various themes involved are human copulation and sexual acts (including sodomy); animal-animal copulation; exhibitionism and nudity; childbirth; death-sexuality-music themes; and shamanic themes.

While it would be gratifying to be able to state unequivocally the exact percentage of Mochica art that features sexual themes, it is impossible to do so. Unfortunately, thousands of ceramics from this culture derive from clandestine excavations and pilferage without any documentation, which is a typical archaeological frustration in Mesoamerica. We can only utilize the documented materials available to us from publications and museum collections to speculate on the important role that such themes play overall in the society.

In the coastal region of Peru, prolonged drought, alterations of sea currents (which bring sea life), and the variant fertility of the seas made life very precarious indeed. *Homo sapiens*, faced with the calamities of nature, the capriciousness of the ocean, and the vagaries of rainfall upon which life depends, was obviously faced with the need to control the fecundity of the environment, particularly the demographic balance or what archaeologists refer to as the carrying capacity of a given econiche. Shamanic leaders were believed to have power of control over the reproduction of animal and plant species upon which their peoples depended. Plant hallucinogens are implicated in shamanic power since we find beliefs in other cultures that plant hallucinogen ingestion permits shamans to transform themselves into the form of powerful animal, plant, and fish familiars over which they have control and which they can beckon to do their bidding (see Dobkin de Rios 1976; Saler 1964).

MOCHICA SEXUAL THEMES AND GROUP SURVIVAL   Examining the categories of sexual themes in art mentioned earlier, we can discuss them in terms of the connection between shamanic activities and group survival. Depictions of human copulation in the large majority seem to involve acts of sodomy. Donnan has noted that none of the Mochica art shows any practice that would lead to insemination and subsequent childbirth. He points out that when details are sufficiently clear, only anal intercourse is shown (1976: 133). Ethnohistorical data indicate that seventeenth-century Catholic priests found sodomic practices prevalent and had instructions from Rome to extirpate such "ungodly" acts. Yet it may be that the representation of sodomy in the religious art of a people (and most art in non-Western societies is linked to religious beliefs and rituals) may be seen as an important mechanism for spacing births in areas where seasonal fluctuations in rainfall, food harvests, available fish resources, and so on, can be crucial (see Kauffmann 1978: 372). Throughout the world, limitations in the carrying capacity of a given environment have demanded from people cultural as well as biological responses. Postpartum sexual abstention of up to three years is a generally cited worldwide average, to ensure that a nursing infant will not die because of malnutrition when his mother becomes pregnant again and another baby displaces him at the breast. Sodomy can be viewed as still another cultural mechanism to achieve spacing of births.

The shaman as psychopomp, and by means of plant hallucinogen ingestion, reaffirms cultural beliefs concerning his control over nature. The art illustrates how this personal shamanic power is enhanced by the type and number of animal familiars represented. By the same token, animal-animal copulation presented in the art also speaks to the issue of shamanic power in that one function of the shaman is to ensure the reproduction and increase of the animals upon which the community depends for its subsistence.

With regard to the third category of ceramics, that of exhibitionism (so-called by Larco [1965]), we find a number of representations of male and female nude figures, some lacking genitalia. Furst (1965) has pointed out that nude figures which

lack genitalia symbolically represent shamanic and religious figures because of the celibacy demands of the role. In cultures
where plant hallucinogens are used, periods of celibacy are generally required for men and women during apprenticeship periods when they may live apart from society in wilderness areas
and experiment with numerous hallucinogenic plants (Dobkin
de Rios 1972b).

From an anatomical point of view, coastal peoples represented the urinary tract in all its morphology—the kidneys, the
pelvis, and the urethra. The male sexual organ was modeled not
only in terms of simple proportions and morphology, but with
anatomical dissections showing the turgid glans and the balano-
preputial sulcus. The representation of the phallus was not realistic in its proportions but merely modeled the erect organ. A
number of Mochica ceramic pieces in the form of male phalli
may indicate a particular sense of humor.

Most of the Mochica ceramics that show mammary glands
feature great detail and indicate the changes that these glands
undergo with age and pregnancy. The female sexual tract, however, was not studied in as detailed a fashion as that of the male.
Mochica artists represented the female sexual tract including the
labia majora and minora and drew the mucous folds covering
the clitoris and posterior commissure (Urteaga-Ballon 1968).
There is some indication in the ethnohistorical writings of the
sixteenth century that the coastal peoples practiced abortion to
interrupt pregnancy, and that they may have practiced Caesa-
rean birth in cases where the mother had died and the child had
to be saved. In the Brunning Museum in Lambayeque, close to
the Mochica area, surgical instruments highly suggestive of di-
lators and curettes may have been used to increase cervical di-
ameters and for uterine curettage (Kauffmann 1978).

Themes of death and sexuality, with musical instruments
present, are another major grouping. Painted motifs of the ceramics show cadavers and skeletonized figures, often with their
genitalia represented or performing fellatio. Only one kiss is
represented in relationship to an animated cadaver—one who
introduces his tongue into the mouth of his female companion.
One ceramic represents a cadaver masturbating. There are nu-

merous ceramics showing animated cadavers with erect penises who are playing musical instruments similar to a reed pan pipe. Cadavers are never represented in the act of heterosexual lovemaking. It is hard to decipher this combination of variables— themes of sexual union, death of one's enemy, the spilling of this blood, and the fecundity of the earth. Throughout the world, where plant hallucinogens are utilized, the motif of death and rebirth, however, is commonly found (see Dobkin de Rios 1975). Additionally, witchcraft connected to love magic is a theme that is frequently found in Peru and has been described by the author in earlier publications (see especially 1972b). In coastal areas, it is believed that witchcraft can be caused by a drink made from the bones of a dead person. Many types of illnesses are believed to arise from love conflicts; for instance, women thought to be immoral prepare a drink (called *pusanga* in the tropical rain forest) which they introduce into a man's refreshment to make him impotent with his wife or consort. The plant hallucinogens play an important role for shamanic healers in diagnosing the cause of evil or disharmony between a man and wife. The shaman's healing role is to identify the source of witchcraft via a vision before he can rectify the damage. Oftentimes, vengeance or envy is the important emotion involved.

Calderón and Sharon (1978) have described coastal witchcraft activities in the Trujillo region (the source of many of the North coast ceramics) where an herb, *huanarpo colorado* (unidentified), turns a man into a "sexual beast" who cannot satisfy his sexual appetites or instincts. The individual can die from excessive inflammation of the genitals. This would correspond to many of the representations of enlarged male phalli found in the art of this region in light of regnant witchcraft and love magic themes present. Eduardo Calderón, a healer studied by Sharon (1972a) in Trujillo, has described the many cases he encountered of individuals who suffered from *daño*, a folk illness that can be related to harmful love magic. As with folk healers throughout Peru, Calderón's clientele often wished him to cure their illnesses, which they believed were due to affective disorders linked to interpersonal conflicts. Calderón used the San Pedro cactus for its visionary properties to see the origin of the witchcraft hex. The materia magica which he used in his San Pedro healing sessions generally included symbolic representations of female genitalia, in this case a sea shell shaped in the form of a vulva. When I conducted fieldwork in a north coast healing village in 1967, healers were quick to offer me, for a fee, retribution for any offense in the area of love that I might wish to rectify.

SHAMANIC THEMES LINKED TO SEXUAL REPRESENTATIONS Many sexual motifs found in ancient Mochica art can be viewed in terms of the consuming cultural focus on the need, by regional leaders, for power over man and nature. Unlike the prelates of religious systems based on more intensive agriculture than the Mochica had, among whom supplication and submission to forces deemed more powerful than themselves was common, shamanic leaders in northern Peru depended mightily upon hallucinogenic brews as a way of consolidating their political and psychological powers. Forces of good and evil were seen to be constantly at issue. The moral order was an overwhelming consideration. The shaman's special relationship to his animal familiars incorporated power, speed, vision, predation, and/or fecundity to his own purposes. While early interpretations of pre-Columbian sexual themes in ceramic art have focused on the "depravity" of ancient peoples, because of their "lascivious" representations of explicit sexual activity, nudity, and/or exhibitionism, I view the art in relation to the use of plant hallucinogens by regional shamanic leaders to facilitate control over fecundity of animal species and the fertility of the land and the sea. While the so-called erotic art of Peru probably represents only a small fraction of the total production of religious art, it gives us insight into a major theme in pre-Columbian coastal civilizations—namely the role of powerful regional political and religious leaders who tried to maintain a balance between the fertility of the land and the sea, on the one hand, and, on the other, the demographic stability necessary for survival.

Turning to other themes in Mochica pottery, we find a link between ideas of death and rebirth prominent in general among drug-using societies. This may be tied to Benson's suggestions of male initiation drug use (1974).

Other Shamanic Themes in Mochica Art

THE SHAMAN AS SPIRITUAL VOYAGER AND DIVINER   Several Mochica ceramics are circular spiral pots that may illustrate the classical shamanistic voyage to nether regions for purposes of communication with the dead or the ancestors, to bring back divinatory messages, or to seek the cause of illness or misfortune (see fig. 22). Benson argues that death haunts all of Mochica art (1972: 152); indeed, this theme may be better interpreted as the common hallucinogen-linked one of death and rebirth. In a study of over 2,000 patients who were administered LSD in psychotherapy, Grof found the death-rebirth subjective effect a frequent one (1972: 51), especially in its spiritual aspects.

Standard interpretations of Mochica pottery turn to the figure of the "bean warrior" in looking for clues to divination. Occasionally, beans are identified with messengers (Sawyer 1966: 50). Although botanical identification is still lacking, a plant known as *camalonga* is used as a hallucinogen in the Peruvian tropical rain forest. The bean is triangular in shape. Among tribal societies, hallucinogenic plant use is often associated with paranormal phenomena, although explanations within a scientific paradigm, to date, are lacking. Figures 23 and 24 indicate a theme that will be discussed shortly, linked to shamanistic metamorphosis into animal or plant familiars. Such metamorphosis, rather than divination, may be a better interpretation of the role of the bean in Mochica art.

THE SHAMAN AND METAMORPHOSIS INTO ANIMAL FAMILIARS   This common drug-linked and pan-American theme in general results in spirit familiars which in Mochica art never appear in battle scenes but are only associated with human beings. A study by Pitt-Rivers (1970) on spiritual power in Central America can be generalized to help us interpret the beliefs linked to hallucinogenic plant use. The author speaks of the term *nagual* (animal familiar) as a prototype, illustrating a type of relationship between an individual man or woman and an animal species. The nagual in Chiapas and parts of Mexico has been shown by Pitt-Rivers to be linked to the spiritual power of an individual. Just

Figure 22. Mochica shamanic voyage to nether worlds. (After Benson 1972: 41)

Figure 23.   Mochica bean warrior. (After Sawyer 1966: 50)

Figure 24.   Metamorphosis of Mochica shaman figure into plant familiar.
(After Kutscher 1950: 181)

as there are differences among naguals in strength, activity, and
power in the world of nature, so too, do the naguals represent
a spiritual hierarchy of individual men and/or women (1970:
187). For example, the jaguar or tiger is more powerful than the
dog, who is more cunning than the raccoon. The animal familiar
has an analogous function in making explicit the relative spiritual power of the shaman. In many Mochica pots, animal familiars are represented in great number and include snakes,
numerous felines, foxes, and so on.

Lavallée's study of Mochica animal representations from
museums and private collections cites forty-four pieces illustrating a frog/toad motif. The hallucinogenic properties of the
toad have been discussed (Erspamer et al. 1967; Daly and Witkop
1971) and seem to have been well known by shamans all
throughout nuclear America. I have cited this phenomenon for
the Maya (1974a and chapter 8) as has Furst (1972) for Indian
America in general (see also Kennedy 1982). The hummingbird,
another frequent motif, may represent both the aerial voyage
and the treating of illness by sucking at afflicted parts of a patient's body (Sharon and Donnan 1974: 54).

The jaguar and eagle as predators, when shown in their
nagual function, may credit their owners with maleficent intentions, while vegetarian animals might not. The nagual could
also indicate the way an individual uses power. Certainly the
parallel between the shamanistic animal familiar and the shaman's warrior nature is not surprising (cf. Benson 1972). Pitt-
Rivers, in his excellent summary article (1970), points out that
dangerous animals and high-flying birds in Central America are
usually reserved as naguals for the mature—in particular, curers.
In many parts of the New World, there is a belief that disease
and misfortune are the outcome of a combat between shamanistic naguals. In curing, a shaman must combat his opponent's
nagual at the same time that he is working on the corporeal
presence of his patient, by sucking, blowing tobacco smoke, and
other techiques. Lavallée cites the widespread myth in South
America that shamans can metamorphize into jaguars (1970:
105). Several Mochica pots photographed by Benson show the
process of metamorphosis or transformation. Benson's recent

study of the feline motif in Mochica art (1974: 9) discusses the portrayal of a trancelike state. The head of the feline is often associated with the Mochica trophy human head, and the paws and head of the feline are always somewhere near the man's head. She suggests, among other alternatives, that a shaman is either in a state of exhilaration or intoxication while hallucinating the feline, or else undergoing initiatory wounding.

Shamans' familiars can also be plants. Camalonga, San Pedro, coca, and Datura are all candidates for a shamanistic transformation following the use of such plants. It is interesting to note in Mochica art that beans are the only vegetable appearing truly anthropomorphized, with a head, arms, and legs. Benson, among others, has suggested that this plant was a representation of a warrior or messenger (1972: 81), although the beans are not rendered in a naturalistic fashion and makes this interpretation difficult to sustain. In fact, they float in the air in various ritual scenes.

When an individual transforms into his nagual, he demonstrates possession of a particularly powerful spiritual nature represented by the animal (Pitt-Rivers 1970: 199). The nagual, then, is part of an analogy system in which the specific animal species defines the social personality of the man vis-à-vis other members of his community. The plant hallucinogens, in this case, serve always as vehicles of transformation and control.

Chapter 8

The Ancient Maya

An examination of ancient Maya art from Mexico, Guatemala, and Belize shows that three art motifs appear with some regularity throughout the archaeological record, from Preclassic through post-Conquest times. These include the mushroom, the frog or toad, and the water lily. All motifs are present in the three major Maya regions, with variations in frequency.

It is my belief that these three motifs are related to, and influenced by, the psychotropic properties of the mushroom, the water lily, and the toad. I argue that the drug properties of these three were known to the Maya shaman, priest, and artist, as well as generally diffused at a folk level in Preclassic times. A major intent of this chapter will be to shed light on the influence of such psychoactive substance use on Maya religion. The first part will examine in general psychoactive substances whose use is documented in this area of the world. The second part will reexamine Maya religion in the light of the possible influence of the psychoactive materials.

Psychoactive Substances in Mesoamerica

THE MUSHROOMS   Present-day Mexico is host to more than 20 species of mind-altering mushrooms, including species of Psilocybe and Stropharia (Heim and Wasson 1958). These mushrooms contain various alkaloids that produce alterations in con-

117

sciousness. In fact, the drug psilocybin, synthesized in recent decades, comes from one of the major alkaloids in the mushroom of similar name. Extant cultic use of these substances among Mixtec, Zapotec, and Mixe populations of Oaxaca has been reported by Wasson and Wasson (1957), Heim and Wasson (1958) and de Borhegyi (1965).

De Borhegyi has written extensively about the corpus of over 100 mushroom stones and ceramics found in southern Mesoamerica and has documented the presence of this motif in both stones and pottery throughout the Guatemalan highlands and parts of the central regions (1961, 1965). Mushroom stones are found in the Early and Preclassic (1650–1050 B.C.) and Late Preclassic (300–50 B.C.) periods at Kaminaljuyu and Quiche and in the Late Preclassic and Early Classic (300 B.C.–A.D. 550) at several sites in the central Guatemalan highlands and the Pacific Coast plains. In addition to the mushroom stones, mushroom pottery is found at a Protoclassic level at El Bellote, Santa Cruz, Chiapa de Corzo, and Mirador. Early Classic pottery mushroom finds can be seen at Berriozabal and at a lowland site, Altar de Sacrificios (de Borhegyi 1963). The time range for pottery mushrooms is Early Preclassic through Late Classic (1650 B.C.–A.D. 800), with a possible hiatus during the Early Classic (A.D. 300–600) (ibid.). The distribution of mushroom stones and pottery mushrooms overlaps into Tabasco, Chiapas, and El Salvador, while mushroom stones are numerous in all parts of highland Guatemala.

Mushrooms are referred to once each in the *Popul Vuh* and the *Annals of the Cakchiquels*, important accounts of the pre-Conquest history and customs of the highland Maya (de Borhegyi 1965). During pre-Columbian times, de Borhegyi has written, pottery mushrooms and mushroom stones were used in sacred ceremonies of the Maya, with ritual consumption of psychotropic mushrooms to induce hallucinatory experience. He has argued that support for cultic associations can be found in the occurrence of many of these plain pottery mushroom-like objects in tombs which contain luxury objects such as carved shell gorgets and jade beads. He points out that these pottery objects are present in areas where stone for carving was abundant and that they were manufactured from local clay and in prevalent local styles. He also writes that in those areas of the Guatemalan highlands where mushroom stones appear from Preclassic times on, no record of hallucinogenic mushrooms is found in plant lists, nor are such practices recorded in the region. According to the Wassons, however, four mushroom stones have been found in Oaxaca, where the hallucinogenic mushroom is still used today, and some of the later archaeological finds of mushroom stones are in parts of Mixe country where modern mushroom use was documented in the late 1950s (Wasson and Wasson 1957).

It is possible that psychotropic mushrooms were important trade items in the southern highlands, where active commerce with other parts of Middle America existed (see McGuire 1982; Brown 1983). Lowe and Mason (1965) have pointed out that the Pacific Coast plain was the principal overland route between Mexico and Central America in pre- and post-Hispanic times. Mixe territory is contiguous, and trade in these psychoactive substances may have occurred. Examples of trade among different areas of Mesoamerica are numerous in the archaeological literature. Eccentric flints, for example, found in the Guatemalan highlands (although rare), are believed to have originated in Guerrero (Thompson 1970). Slate, too, may have been exported from the Pacific Coast around Sacapulas to the highlands (ibid.). Thompson pointed out that trade in pottery between various parts of the Maya area, and even with non-Maya regions, was brisk even as early as Preclassic. Early Classic burials in Kaminaljuyu contain many trade pieces from Central Mexico (Thompson 1954). Glazed pumbate ware depicting Mexican gods was traded throughout southern Guatemala. Early Classic thin orange pottery ware ranged as far afield as Kaminaljuyu, Teotihuacan, and Monte Alban; Thompson believes this pottery type to have been manufactured in Central Mexico. It is quite possible that some of these trade goods were accompanied by psychotropic mushrooms as items offered for exchange, or that the mushrooms themselves were trade items.

To bolster the argument that mushroom stones and ceramics indicate use of the psychotropic mushrooms themselves, de Borhegyi (1965) suggested that the use of aromatic pine resins for magical and religious ritual may be connected with such use. Throughout the so-called primitive world where similar hallucinogenic drugs are used, odoriferous plants play an important part in heightening sensory responses during drug experiences. Elsewhere, I have pointed out the use of perfumed water (*agua florida*) in ayahuasca sessions (see chapter 12). It is interesting in this context that when the mushroom motif disappears from the archaeological record, so does the three-pronged *incensario* container in which pine resins were burned (de Borhegyi 1965).

THE FROG/TOAD MOTIF   Bufotenine, derived from the poison of the toad, has for the past few decades been a subject of experimentation among both human and primate populations (see Evarts 1956; Fabing and Hawkins 1956; Fabing 1957). An indole substance, it has been known as an adrenergic agent since its isolation by Wieland in 1934. In 1954, this substance was found in the seed of *Anadenanthera perigrina*, the *cohoba* snuff of the West Indies (Stowe 1959). Bufotenine is a hallucinogenic drug which has dangerous cardiovascular and central nervous system effects in man, and is usable only in low dosages. Its passage through the blood-brain barrier, however, is still unclear. Some writers believe that hydroxy derivatives such as bufotenine do not have to penetrate the brain all the way, but only as far as some trigger point like the hypothalamus, in order to produce regional changes (Szara, cited in Efron 1967). Wassen (1934) and others have traced the importance of the frog/toad motif in New World art, but to my knowledge, aside from an oblique reference to Shakespearean-type witches' brews and the use of toads therein, at the time Wassen wrote the article no attempt had been made to link the frog/toad motif with the biochemical data. My argument in this chapter clearly depends upon the indentification of the toad, not the frog, as the major figure in art representations. Some substantiation for my argument can be seen in the various analyses available of the codices and the works of art themselves. The importance of the frog has, in fact, been reviewed recently by Kennedy (1982).

Tozzer and Allen (1910), in a study of animal figures in the Maya codices, use the terms *frog* and *toad* interchangeably, believing that it is never quite clear which of these related rain-associated amphibians is meant by the artist. They argue, indeed, that no distinction in treatment is made between the two and find it impossible to identify these representations positively with any of the numerous species of frog or toad that occur in Central America. The Maya word used for this motif (*uo*) is found in several places in the codices and stone carvings. Furst has presented the symbolic properties of the toad as "earth mother" in Mesoamerican mythology and art, especially with regard to the toad's properties of metamorphosis—the cycle of death and regeneration which may, in the long run, be more important in interpreting ancient Mayan art than a focus on disputed biochemical properties of bufo poisons (see Schultes and Hofmann 1973).

It is interesting to note an 1898 report of Maya whistles with frog representations. These may have been used in hallucinogenic contexts. The role of auditory stimulation in hallucinogenic experience has been relatively neglected, but is of great importance in understanding how a drug session is guided (see Katz and Dobkin de Rios 1971; Dobkin de Rios and Katz 1975; Stat 1974).

Other instances of the toad motif can be found in the Madrid Codex, which contains representations of tree amphibians known for their loud voices during the rainy season. Tozzer and Allen link the presence of these amphibians to their importance to gods associated with the agricultural seasons and the sowing of grain at the beginning of the rainy period. Shellhas (1904) has pointed out that the "frog" god, pictured with the club-shaped fins of a frog in the Madrid Codex, is shown sowing seed and making furrows with a planting stick.

Landa (1941), writing of festivities during the second Maya month *uo*, which falls at the height of the rainy season, spoke of a dance at the end of a period of drunkenness called *Okot uil*. Tozzer notes that the literal translation of this term is the "dance of the moon or month." He also cites Roys's suggestion that *uil* is a contraction of *uoil* (*uinal uo*), "of the frogs."

Greene (1967) reports that the Tablet of the Palace in Palenque, c. A.D. 645, contains a glyph detail showing the figure of a toad, which she says represents the Maya month of *uo*. She sees the principal attribute of the sculpture to be the toad poison gland, which is represented by three circles at the back of its head.

An important function for the frog or toad was as the musician and guest of the Chacs, the Yucatec rain gods. Four in number, the Chacs are found, in art, attended by small amphibians whose croaking announces rain (Thompson 1954). Morley (1956) argues that these four representations are aspects of a single rain deity. Thompson (1970) reproduces a part of the Madrid Codex in which water pours earthward from the anus of a Chac; the god is surrounded by four frogs or toads, which also spout water. Thompson argued that the Chac cult was limited to Yucatan, where it was probably very old; in the highlands of Guatemala and Chiapas, the gift of rain is seen to be in the hands of the mountain or earth gods. Thompson cites the connection between the rain gods and lightning and thunderbolts; according to the Motul Dictionary, the Chac was a man of great stature who taught agriculture and whom the Indians held to be the god of bread and water, thunder and lightning—in short, the god of the milpa, or farmland. Since the frog/toad announces rain, the intimate relationship with the god is clear.

At Kaminaljuyu, in Tomb I, Mound E-III-3, there is an interesting combination of materials connected with the frog/toad and the mushroom motifs. The pottery collection includes a quantity of black/brown fine-incised standard shallow bowls (over 300 specimens) with a quadruped motif (Shook and Kidder 1952). In their figure 19 in particular, a pottery vessel in the form of a frog or toad is presented. Cylindrical or goblet-type vessels with similar quadrupedal figures, which may have been used to imbibe a drink or some unknown psychoactive substance, were also found. In addition, Shook and Kidder picture what they call a toad bowl in figure 35, although the identification of the toad is not certain. Shook and Kidder mention Shepard's identification of the boss on some of the pottery vessels as originating from the poison gland of a common Middle American species of toad. They note that an amphibian, whether toad or frog, was the harbinger of rain and was venerated by those who equipped Tomb I during the Preclassic period. Also included in the tomb's contents were several small toad or frog mortars of gray stone, mushroom stones of coarse-grained lava, and a tripod mushroom stone with a jaguar head. De Borhegyi (1961) argues that these were burial offerings. Shook and Kidder suggest that the richness of the Tomb I finds indicates the burial of a personage of wealth; from the evidence just cited, the individual would appear to have been a shaman or priest. It is interesting that this tomb was robbed, but only partially, shortly after it was laid down. Perhaps the grave-robbers realized that the tomb was of an important shaman or priest and quickly withdrew. Elsewhere in the same cemetery, a cache of nine mushroom stones was found in association with nine miniature manos and metates. De Borhegyi argues that those, too, were burial offerings; he suggests that the metates and mortars were used to crush psychoactive mushrooms or *ololiuqui* (morning glory) seeds to be taken for their visionary properties. De Borhegyi points to sixteenth-century Spanish chroniclers' reports (cited in Wasson and Wasson [1957]) of hallucinatory visions of jaguars, gods, and snakes as well as little gnomelike creatures which he argues may have been coded as gods of the underworld. The presence of ololiuqui in Mexico has been reported by Schultes (1941), although no cultural activity connected with it has ever been mentioned in the literature.

Another interesting linkage of a mushroom and toad comes from the modern Quiche area, where an unwholesome mushroom is called *holom ixpek*, "toad's head" (Wasson and Wasson 1957). This kind of linkage between the two is widely documented by the authors for Indo-European languages.

There are many other toad representations that could be cited, ranging from Chalchuapa, El Salvador, to Izapa and Tonala, Chiapas, to Kaminaljuyu. Rands (1953, 1955) has discussed the iconic representation of the linkages between the jaguar, toad, and serpents in the Altar A at Copan in terms of mythological beliefs connected with this sculpture, which was seen to represent heavenly forces always engaged in battle. The serpent rain god is most important, but in times of destructive floods, the dry-weather god, the jaguar, must be involved. Spinden,

Rands points out, has identified the jaguar as the god of the clear sky and the serpent as the god of the clouded sky, storm, lightning, rain, and the wet season.

It is clear that the Maya could have used the skin or poison glands from the common *Bufo marinus* toad, or some other species, in religious activity, but it is impossible to demonstrate that they did. Mackenzie (1924) has written that Aztec rites existed in which priests and others entered a lake and swallowed live water-snakes and frogs. The goddess Chalchiuhtilicue was sometimes depicted as a frog, and jadite frogs were favored amultets. Motolinia, in his cited history of the Indians of New Spain, wrote that the Indians of the New World had numerous idols including frogs and even toads (cited in Braden 1930). It is not surprising that the ethnohistorical materials should offer us so few clues as to the use of psychotropic substances. Schultes, among others (1970), pointed out that native beliefs related to psychoactive drug use evoked only the scorn and distaste of the Spanish conquerors, which resulted in the driving underground of many psychotropic substances.

THE WATER LILY   The common water lily is an aquatic plant of the genus *Nymphaea*. An African representative of this genus, *Nymphaea caerula sav.*, is used as a narcotic among African groups (William Emboden, personal communication). Although biochemical identification of the New World variety (*N. ampla;* fig. 25) has not been attempted, it is a generally valid assumption that if psychotropic properties exist in one member of a genus, they will probably be found in others. The pharmacologist Farnsworth (personal communication) wrote that the lotus plant, which plays an important part in Asian art and is also a member of the *Nymphaeaceae,* contains opiate-like alkaloids. Ekholm and Heine-Geldern (cited in Rands 1953) have pointed out the similarity in art representations of the water lily between Buddhist and Maya art and have explained this similarity as due to trans-Pacific contacts. The botanical data suggest, rather, that such similarity may be related to the intrinsic properties of the plants in question.

Rands (1953, 1955) has listed the following major sites for the presence of the water lily motif in the Maya area: Quirigua,

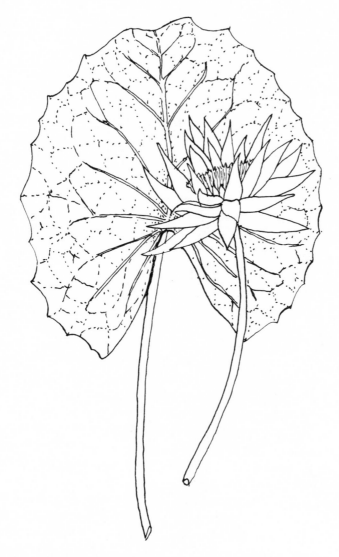

Figure 25. Nymphaea ampla. (*After Emboden 1979: 51*)

Copan, Chichen Itza, Yaxchilan, Santa Rita, Tulum, Tikal, Palen, Kaminaljuyu, Bonampak (murals), Usumacinta, and Piedras Negras. In addition, the Dresden Codex has numerous representations of the water lily. Most of the dates would appear to fall within the Classic period, although aside from stone monuments, the motif is difficult to date. The only ceramic evidence cited by Rands for water lily motifs comes from Alta Verapaz (1953).

Rands has described the mythic associations of the lily as follows:

1. Death symbols are recurrent.
2. Mythic beings occur as the source of the plant, and include the long-nosed serpent or rain god, a bird form, and the jaguar.
3. The anatomical areas found in association with the lily are the top of the head, the ears, eyes, mouth, hands, and perhaps the neck and nose regions. This is suggestive of the effects that psychotropic substances have upon all sensory modes.
4. At Palenque, the maize god is found in association with elaborate stems or vines of the lily, which pass through his hand.
5. In the Dresden Codex, the water lily is found in the hand of the long-nosed god. Suggestions of paraphernalia are also found. This may indicate preparation of the plant either in a drink or in powdered form to facilitate contact with the supernatural.
6. At Palenque, the lily is associated with one of the nine lords of the underworld.
7. At Copan, the lily is associated with the toad on Stela D and Zoomorph B.
8. Like the lotus in Asian art, the water lily of the Maya is shown with its stem emerging from a human figure's mouth and its stalk held in the hands. Reclining human figures are often placed amidst the plants. If, indeed, both the water lily and the lotus possess narcotic properties, then such visual representations do not appear to

be strange at all; one would not have to postulate trans-Pacific contacts to explain them.

Rand speculates that the Usumacinta region may have been the area in which the water lily motif received its highest elaboration, although no early period representations of the plant are definitely known. However, from the middle of the Classic period until the beginning of the Mexican period, especially at Chichen Itza, the water lily motif is very common. Rands saw this motif as part of a complex of beliefs connected with the maize plant and one that was important in Maya religious symbolism.

At this point it is important to tell the story of the discovery of startling new information concerning the drug properties of the water lily. In an earlier version of this chapter, written in 1971, I suggested that the ancient Maya used *Nymphaea ampla* in healing activities; before the article was published in 1974, I discussed my findings with archaeologists at the University of California, Berkeley. Before the article's publication in 1974, Diaz, a biochemically oriented medical researcher at the National University of Mexico, learned that young American visitors to highland Chiapas in 1973 were using the rhizomes of the plant as a recreational drug. Diaz began gas chromatographic studies of the plant and showed that it contained aporphine, which is related chemically to apomorphine (a highly emetic morphine-like substance). Emboden, following this research lead, has published a number of papers on the role of the water lily in the art and religion of ancient Egypt (Emboden 1981, 1982; Emboden and Dobkin de Rios 1981). While Emboden and I in our 1982 paper were unable to make specific suggestions as to exact healing rituals in either Mayan or Egyptian civilizations, it was important to note some unusual drug properties of the plant. Clinically speaking, apomorphine has a long history of use in Western culture as an emetic, which causes heavy and continuous vomiting. Such a drug effect, at first blush, might appear to have been inimical to the religious experience sought after by the Mayan priest at a temple center. Yet after the apomorphine's emetic effect wears off, a dreamy, languid period follows. Apomorphine also has proven therapeutic effects among mentally ill patients.

The historian of medicine E. Ackerknecht has argued that throughout the world, societies that believe in witchcraft and supernatural etiology of disease also acknowledge the role of object intrusion, taking the form of a thorn or dart from evil magicians. Such societies clearly would recognize the symbolic importance of any drug that creates altered states of consciousness by means of vomitive therapeutics. It may be that the effects of one of the alkaloids present in the lily, nupharidine, indicate that the plant plays an important role in contributing to the hypnotic state so important to New World shamanic cognitions and behavior (see Dobkin de Rios 1976).

Maya Religion and Psychotropic Drug Use

Maya religion developed from the shamanic level of Protoclassic times to a sociocultural level that included a hierarchy of religious officials or priests, served by various assistants such as artisans and craftsmen (Vogt and Ruz Lhuillier 1964). Shamans and priests existed simultaneously among the classic Maya, each with different and complementary methods of recruitment, training, and ritual function. There were ceremonial centers, which may have been controlled by sets of permanent priests/ rulers with inherited positions emerging in fully developed aristocratic lineages. In fact, from scholarship like that of Tatiana Proskouriakoff on the dated monuments from Piedras Negras (as cited in Coe 1966), it appears that much Classic relief sculpture represented dynastic autocrats, their families, and various important events during their reigns. These autocrats were probably the ones who carried on various aspects of the hieratic tradition and depended, in turn, upon the ordinary Maya peasants' labor to produce corn, the important staple. In addition, the peasantry in outlying hamlets would have been in relatively constant contact with ceremonial centers, attending and participating in religious ceremonies and trade.

While the priests who occupied the ceremonial centers were responsible for the operation of centers, ceremonials, and calendars, there were shaman-like curanderos at the folk level who may have functioned to diagnose illness and to perform curing ceremonies for individuals. They were believed to have derived their power from dreams or other vision-like experiences. It is important to stress here that in nonliterate societies, hallucinogenic plant users insist upon the powers ensuing from such plant use. I would argue that once such substances were usurped by hieratic functionaries, their use would be strictly controlled and forbidden to local shamans. In a state-level society, power to bewitch through access to drugs would be a threat to "legitimate power" and individual drug-users would be viewed as dangerous. Prior to the Inca consolidation of sedentary agricultural village-level society, for example, coca appears to have been widely used; the Inca forbade the use of the substance to any but the Inca and his court, and myths were promulgated telling how the gods gave coca to the Inca as the source of his power (Taylor 1966).

Many of the techniques for extracting psychoactive substances from plants or animals may have been developed at the folk level, which I am relating here to Preclassic periods. If, indeed, as La Barre argues (1970), an incipient narcotic complex existed in Siberia, we may speculate that there was a similar predisposition among PaleoIndian hunter/gatherers to utilize mushrooms and similar plants that they found in their New World foraging. Wasson and Wasson (1957) make a basic distinction between mycophilia and mycophobia, given the fact that many diverse peoples do not consider mushrooms edible. With the predisposition among New World populations to utilize mushrooms as food (as well as drugs), it is possible to speculate that the psychoactive mushrooms may have played an important role in southern Mesoamerican life. Lévi-Strauss (1970) has shown the distribution of American Indian use of mushrooms as food outside Mexico to include the following tribal groups: California Indians, Salish, Kwakiutl, Menomini, Blackfoot, Omaha, Iroquois, Ge, Mundurucu, Yurimagua, Tukuna, Jicarilla Apache, and the Argentine Toba.

From a pragmatic point of view, we can be sure that mushroom use is very old. While many other psychoactive substances must be boiled, pulverized, and specially prepared before their alkaloid properties are released, psychotropic mushrooms can be used both raw and dried, later reconstituted with a bit of water; hence they probably entered the hunter's repast more easily than cultivated plants.

A search of Maya ethnographies in modern times fails to bring forth evidence of modern use of the toad, except for one reference among the Chorti, who use the frog to extract disease symbolically from a sick person (Reina 1969). As has also been mentioned, mushroom use in modern Maya areas is non-existent. If the use of various psychoactive flora and fauna developed, was elaborated at the folk level, and was subsequently incorporated into hieratic cult use, such practices may well have gone underground at the time of Mexican incursions into Maya land and the subsequent Spanish conquest, when the use of psychoactive drugs in Mexico was systematically eradicated. With regard to toad utilization, in particular, it may very well be that the esoteric knowledge necessary to extract minute quantities of a very poisonous substance disappeared along with the specialized groups who utilized this technique. As with the Maya system of hieroglyphics and calendrics, little has remained in recorded history, and such knowledge has had to be reevaluated in subsequent centuries.

MAIZE AND THE CHAC   The importance of maize in Maya subsistence and the personification of the rain god, Chac, as a vital force of nature may be connected to the use of psychoactive substances. The Chac occurs 218 times in the three codices (Morley 1956) and is viewed by Morley and Thompson as one of the most important deities for the Maya farmer. Thompson saw this cult as very ancient, occurring in the monuments of the Classic period and in the Yucatec codices. As has been pointed out, the frog/toad was viewed as the messenger and guest of the Chac. If the Chac did not send rain, perhaps a priest would imbibe a potion of his messenger's substance in order to enter into more direct communication with the omnipotent forces controlling his destiny. If we view magical rites as an attempt to control the unknown, then utilization of powerful hallucinogenic substances might make the supernatural more accessible to the priest, whose role it was to oversee the agricultural activities of the populace and to utilize his powers for communal well-being.

TIME   Although many early civilizations have had great interest in astronomy, geometry, divination, and other specialized skills that are involved in the controlling and predicting of agricultural tasks, it may be that the Mayas' focus on the infinity of time can be related to the psychoactive properties of the plants they may have used. Maya preoccupation with marking passages of time was quite distinctive—an all-consuming interest, as Thompson has pointed out. All stelae and altars were erected to mark the passage of time and were dedicated at the end of a particular period. The eternity of time is a common Maya motif. Their concern with time which had no beginning and their interest in past time at the expense of future time is important to consider in light of psychoactive drug influence. Arnold Ludwig has noted the influence of psychoactive substances on time perception. Early anthropological reports of one hallucinogen, ayahuasca, frequently mention the aerial voyage, the feeling that one is floating in an ephemeral time-space continuum unlike anything known in normal waking hours. These phenomena may have convinced the Maya priest that supernatural forces and time itself were cyclical and sacred. It is unfortunate that we have no written records from the Nazca or the Mochica periods to allow us to see to what degree those cultures' obsession with time could be related, if at all, to drug ingestion.

SPIRIT-COMPANIONS   The Maya belief in two kinds of souls or spirits possessed by the individual (the so-called nagual belief described by Vogt and Ruz [1964]) is similar to beliefs of other Indians of the Americas. In Mesoamerica this animal spirit-companion is believed to live apart, although it has an intimate relationship to a man or woman. It is also related to ancestral gods. Vogt and Ruz have written that a person's life depends upon the well-being of his animal counterpart. In drug-using groups from Venezuela to Ecuador, it is believed that upon the intake of the hallucinogenic substance and by means of incantation or whistling, a shaman can call upon spirit protectors or helpers to effect a cure or to control an enemy or a sorcerer attempting evil. Often these creatures are viewed as giants or as small humanoid beings, and can probably be related to the physiological phenomena known as macropsia and micropsia (seeing things large or small) which can occur in the wake of drug use.

DUALISM   Maya religious beliefs have strong dualistic tendencies (e.g., in the eternal struggle between good and evil powers over man, the benevolence and malevolence of the gods, and the conflicting forces within man himself). The emotional extremes of euphoria and anguish released in man by the use of hallucinogenic substances is a possible predisposing factor in this dualism. An artifact described by Stromsvik (cited in Rands 1955: 362) at Copan shows this dualism clearly in the struggle between a jaguar and a serpent god. Use of a psychoactive substance may have been the way in which the magician or sorcerer believed himself able to control unknown forces, either for personal or communal ends. Wasson and Wasson (1957) have argued that hallucinogen use is a major factor in explaining the demons and gods which have entered into man's beliefs throughout the world.

Perhaps the Maya belief in the thirteen worlds of heaven and the nine worlds of hell, and the passage of the gods from one to the other, can be related to some of the phenomena experienced by the drug user. One major aspect of the alteration of visual perception in drug use is that visual images often remain present for a time as new ones are superimposed. This pattern might take on special significance if a shaman were to take a drug while surrounded by ritual objects, perhaps giving rise in him to complex feelings about the transformation of one substance into another. An illustration of this is the "toad" framing a human being in Quirigua which may be a representation of the animal familiar linked with its human shape in the process of shape shifting. As we have noted, Rands has associated the water lily motif with death, and the theme of death and resurrection is very common among drug-using populations.

The association of demonic representations in drug experiences with Maya gods of the underworld does not in any way mean that we should attribute a "bad trip" to the drug-using priest. Rather, cultural patterning of visual drug experience consistently gives rise to a hallucinogenic content which has cultural tuition (Dobkin de Rios 1972b). If beliefs exist concering demon-like gods, a drug-using priest may indeed find himself in contact with a series of forces (both within himself and valued by his culture) which he may attempt to control, or he may see himself as a mouthpiece of the gods of the underworld. In most drug-using cultures prior to Western contact, the notion of a calling is usually acknowledged for the shaman or priest. In those drug-using societies for which we have adequate data, the shaman is generally recognized as a special individual whose nervous system and level of maturity permit him to deal most competently with the realm of unconscious activity generated by hallucino-genic plant use.

DIVINATION   Thompson (1954: 286) has described a Yucatec ritual in which the *chilan* (a special individual who has made prophesies after consulting a divinatory almanac) retired to his house and entered a trance in which he received messages from a god. Thompson believed that the *chilan*'s visions were induced by a narcotic, but he is not sure what drug may have been involved. He suggests tobacco (see fig. 26), whose use is dis-cussed at length by Robicsek (1978). It is possible that an infusion of the rhizome of the water lily or the venom of the toad was used to enable the *chilan* to gain entry into a state of conscious-ness in which he believed that he was serving as a mouthpiece for the gods. The use of hallucinogens for divinatory purposes, as Thompson points out, would not have been unusual, con-sidering the widespread interest in divination among many tribal populations who use powerful mind-altering plants (see Cooper 1949).

Conclusions

Recently Furst and Coe (1977) have pointed out an addi-tional way in which plant hallucinogens could have been ad-ministered among the Maya: by means of enemas, which are portrayed in the art. In their article, these authors express a firm conviction that plant hallucinogens or toad venom were in use by the ancient Maya. This chapter, too, has argued that Maya

Figure 26.   Maya god of tobacco. (After Robicsek 1978: 116)

134

religious beliefs and practices may have been influenced by psychotropic substances portrayed in the art.

It is unusual for independent verification to occur in the social sciences as it might in biomedical areas. I suggested in the original version of my research on the Maya that psychoactive properties of the water lily plant could be inferred from the art; the independent verification by Diaz of the mind-altering properties of this plant is unusual and unexpected. While there is a difference chemically between apomorphine and aporphine, scientists like Emboden are certain of their similar effects. (Compare the string of amines in over-the-counter diet pills. As one combination is placed under medical controls, other alternates appear on the market.)

It is only by examining neighbors of the Maya, the Aztec, that we can see how recorded drug use in that society resembled Maya drug use.

Chapter 9

The Aztecs of Mexico

The Aztecs of ancient Mexico are one of the most interesting hallucinogenic-drug using societies for which there are data. An urban civilization based on irrigation agriculture, with stratification and complex forms of political organization, the Aztec were a warfaring group whose empire was held together by a system of unsteady alliances and power politics. The Aztec civilization achieved hegemony over neighboring geographical areas prior to the Spanish arrival in the New World in the sixteenth century. When the Spanish arrived in Mesoamerica, the Aztecs were still very much involved in the process of consolidating their empire.

Aztec society was comprised of a nonhereditary nobility, a patriciate of priests and high functionaries, and an intermediary group of merchants-entrepreneurs. An enormous peasant mass tilled the soil and was occupied with crafts. Some estimates of pre-Columbian populations are as high as ten million people. In many ways, the achievements of the Aztec civilization were comparable to those of ancient Egypt and Babylonia. Fine cities and broad avenues, stepped pyramids, monumental sculpture, and sumptuous residential palaces amazed the Spanish conquerors (see Ribiero 1971).

The Aztecs used four hallucinogenic drugs not only as a

means to communicate with the supernatural, but as an important part of their war-related activities and as part of their human
sacrifical ceremonies. To some degree, as we shall see shortly,
plant hallucinogens played an important role in facilitating political alliances between great states which made up the confed-
erated Aztec empire. An important group of clergy were engaged
in religious activities and were in control of hallucinogenic drug
use.

The Aztec viewed themselves as the people of the sun, and
by means of human sacrifices, they attempted to propitiate their
sun god. Much of their warfare was devoted to capturing human
beings whom they could offer to their blood-thirsty deity. Human sacrifice was most important during the last 200 years of
their empire, and their warfare and religion were intricately
connected. Certain plant hallucinogens were used to lighten the
pain of captives and to make them oblivious to their fate (Cook
1946). Harner (1977) has argued that cannibalism in Aztec society
was widespread among the populace due to a lack of adequate
protein resources.

Aztec Plant Use

The Aztec used peyote, a small, spineless cactus which contains various alkaloids, including mescaline. Peyote was believed to cause an intoxication lasting from two to three days:
those who ate it were reported to see visions that either frightened them or made them laugh (Perez de Barradas 1950).

A series of hallucinogenic mushrooms, members of the *Stropharia* and *Psilocybe* genuses, were called *teonanacatl*, or "god's
flesh," and played an important part in Aztec ritual life. The
Spanish described three different mushrooms and likened their
effects to wine. The first kind was reputed to cause madness,
with the individual experiencing uncontrollable laughter as part
of the intoxication. On some occasions, it was even written that
this caused a lasting effect. The mushroom was deep yellow in
color, acrid in taste, and was used only when in a fresh state,
not dried. A second mushroom did not induce laughter, but
evoked many different kinds of visions, such as wars and de-

mons. The third group was valued by Aztec nobles for festivals and banquets. Tezozomoc, an early writer, wrote about the costliness of these mushrooms and the all-night vigils required to find them. They were tawny in color and acrid to taste. They were never cooked, but eaten raw, and caused strange hallucinations and colored dreams. They were accompanied by experiences of hilarity, excitation, and at times demonic visions, torpor, and feelings of well-being. They were believed to excite peoples' sexual desires. Some people reported to the Spanish clergy that the mushrooms made a person see snakes and various other visions (Schultes 1960).

The third category of hallucinogens that the Aztec used contained several Datura species of the Nightshade family, which were valued for the drowsiness they invoked. Used for healing, as a local anesthetic, they were called *toloache*. Morning glory seeds (see fig. 27), called *ololiuqui*, were the fourth favorite plant hallucinogen of the Aztec. Called the "green snake weed," perhaps because of its climbing properties, this vision-inducing, lentil-like seed of the vine was esteemed as a divine messenger which transported man into spiritual realms. Those who used ololiuqui were described as being deprived of their reason; their visual hallucinations permitted them to communicate with their deities. The plant possessed certain analgesic properties as well, which explains its common use as a medicine. For gout, it was ground up and applied to the affected part of the body (Schultes 1941).

Some Historical Data

The Aztecs used hallucinogenic plants for many centuries, although we shall never really know just how far back in time one can date their rich drug pharmacopoeia. Some writers believe that peyote was discovered by a group called the Otomi in the northern valleys. The Aztecs themselves were a nomadic and barbarian group who arrived in the Valley of Mexico only some two hundred years before the Spanish conquest. The Nahuas, a people who were then living in the Valley of Mexico, were quite advanced in their cultural development. Their divin-

Figure 27. Rivea corymbosa. (*After Schultes 1941*)

ity, Quetzalcoatl, was a man of wisdom who gave them a code of ethics and a love for art and science. The Nahua groups were preceded in the Valley of Mexico by the Toltec civilization. The Aztec, bellicose and imperialistic compared to their Nahual neighbors, conquered the surrounding groups. Like the Romans, they incorporated the region's native gods into their pantheon, taking on the worship of Quetzalcoatl and his myths and traditions: they adopted his name to denote their most important priest. The Toltecs, who were oriented toward medicinal problems and their resolution (Toro 1954), left the Aztecs a fine body of knowledge gained from their study of herbs.

Scholars believe that as far back as 300 B.C. the Chichimecas, the original Aztec group, as well as the Toltecs, were acquainted with several of the drug plants. One Spanish friar, Sahagun, suggests that peyote gave the Aztecs the courage to fight and the freedom from fear, hunger, and thirst. The Aztecs believed that the plant protected them from all danger. Peyote came from the far northern deserts of Mexico and present-day Texas. The Aztec inhabitants of the Valley of Mexico knew the plant in its preserved state, since it was dried and transported several hundred miles to the south (Safford 1916).

Aztec Religion and Hallucinogen Use

The Aztecs were a polytheistic people. The idea of magical, impersonal, and occult forces was very much present in the minds of their hierarchical functionaries. A numerous class of priests and priestesses specialized in the cults of the gods. They interpreted the divinities and performed rites and ceremonies to propitiate these forces. The regular or legally constituted clergy was in sharp competition with diviners, a group that was heir to a collection of ancient practices in magic. Their empirical knowledge of the curative properties of plants caused others to believe that they possessed supernatural powers (Caso 1958). The masses of people had great faith in these diviners, who probably used hallucinogens in their activities as well. The power that plants were believed to bestow upon the taker would be called upon to summon spiritual forces to one's aid. The

Polynesian term *mana* is useful here to describe the belief that the individual who imbibed a sacred plant would become possessed of its powers and could then control the spirit of the plant for good or evil ends. Thus plants could be used by priestly groups to discern witchcraft, to cure illness, and to predict the future. By the same token, such plants could be used to cause harm to an enemy by means of marshaling all of the plant's presumed power.

We know that during the coronation feast of Montezuma in 1502, *teonanacatl* (the divine mushroom) was used to celebrate the event. War captives were slaughtered in great numbers to honor Montezuma's accession to the throne. Their flesh was eaten, and a banquet was prepared after the victims' hearts were offered to the gods. After the sacrifice was over, everyone was bathed in human blood. Raw mushrooms were given to the guests, which one writer, Fray Durán (1964), described as causing them to go out of their minds—in a worse state than if they had drunk a great quantity of wine. In his description (cited in Schultes 1941), these men were so inebriated that many took their own lives. They had visions and revelations about the future, and Durán thought the devil was speaking to them in their madness. When the mushroom ceremony ended, the invited guests left.

Montezuma invited rival rulers to feasts which were held three times a year. One of these important feasts was called the Feast of Revelations, when the invited dignitaries and Montezuma, or his representative, ate the wild mushrooms. The Spanish, writing about the effects of the mushrooms, always conjured up the devil, but we shall really never know if the Aztecs were seeing anything like the Christian devil. Their visions may indeed have been spirits of their pantheon with whom they were in communication. Sacred mushrooms played such an important part in Aztec life that Indian groups which owed tribute to the Aztec emperor paid it with inebriating mushrooms (Schultes 1940). One Spanish priest wrote that for the Aztecs, the sacred mushrooms were like the host in the Christian religion: through this bitter nourishment, "they received their God in communion" (ibid.).

The divinatory properties of various hallucinogens were of paramount importance to the Aztecs. They believed that whoever ate these sacred plants would receive the power of second sight and prophecy. Thus, one could discover the identity of a thief, find stolen objects, or predict the outcome of a war or the attack of a hostile group. One Spanish botanist and chronicler, Hernández, sent by Philip II of Spain, wrote that the priests ate the morning glory seeds to communicate with their gods and to receive messages from them. By means of inducing a delirium, they received thousands of visions and hallucinations. The plant's divinatory powers were viewed as most important to the priests. Sorcerers used this plant to harm people whom they didn't like. A deity was believed to reside in its seeds, and thus, by ingesting the plant, the oracular power it possessed would come to the taker (Schultes 1970). The divine mushroom was taken during ritual ceremonies. The Florentine Codex records that when the participants ate the mushrooms with honey, and they began to take effect, the Aztecs danced, wept, and saw hallucinations. Others entered their houses in a serious manner and sat nodding. Visions included prophecies of one's own death, battle scenes, or war captives that one would take in battle. Others reported visions that they would be rich. All that could possibly happen to a person could be seen under the effects of the mushrooms. After the effect wore off, people would consult among themselves and tell each other about their visions.

The mushrooms were often part of festivities commemorating victory in battle or the coronation of kings. They were used to solemnize occasions, and often they cemented bonds of friendship between potential enemies. Durán (1964) mentions an occasion of this type, when the Aztecs waged war against a group called Metztitlan and lost more men than they captured. After the war, they invited rulers from neighboring states and made great supplies of food available for feast. The Aztec king was named Tizoc. During his enthronement feast, all those present ate wild mushrooms—the kind that made men lose their senses. After four days of feasting, the newly crowned Tizoc gave his guests rich gifts and sacrificed the Metztitlan victims.

When the Spanish arrived in Mexico in the sixteenth century, they persecuted those priests and practitioners who used the sacred plants in religious rituals. Whatever the visionary effects that informants attributed to the various hallucinogens, these prelates concluded that the devil himself was involved. The Spanish priests, to our knowledge, never used the drugs themselves, and could only speak with disbelief at the reports they collected from informants. Many ecclesiastics were vehemently opposed to the various hallucinogenic plants used by the Aztecs because of the religious importance that the natives gave to these drugs. Although the Aztecs viewed many of the plants as divine messengers, capable of transporting man into spiritual realms, to the Spanish these very attributes impeded their own missionary activity and ability to gain souls for Christ. It is no wonder that they opposed the use of the plants with such determination, while maintaining an open mind concerning other plants with proven medicinal value.

The Spanish, culturally mycophobic to begin with, showed great disgust at seeing these mushrooms in use. In Roman Catholicism, communion with the supernatural is based not upon an individual's revealed knowledge, but rather upon his memberhsip in a complex hierarchical structure and his faith in its doctrines. The individual's relationship with the spiritual world is mediated by priests, and any personal mystical relationship, even within the context of Christianity, has always been viewed with some suspicion by the authorities. Moreover, Aztec belief that the powers residing in the plants could be controlled by the drug user was totally alien to Western thought. Thus the basic magical assumptions inherent in drug use, which portrayed man as capable of controlling the unknown and of using his sacred plants to obtain "power," which he could then use for good or evil purposes, were totally contrary to Christian concepts. In Christian tradition, man's role was that of a supplicant before a much higher spiritual authority. Indeed, one might argue that the loathing that the Spanish held for Aztec sacred plant use was due to this basic clash of theologies and religious structures, as opposed to a mere distrust of the plants themselves. There is good evidence that during the European Middle Ages, various hallucinogenic plants such as Henbane, Mandrake, and Belladonna were used in witches' potions; certainly they were part of the Spanish pharmacopoeia.

Although the Spanish immensely disliked the Aztec use of sacred plants and the Spanish priests did not use them, the Spanish conquistadores were not averse to using certain plants when it suited their own needs. One story is told that Cortez used peyote in Tlaxcala for his auxiliary troops in order to lighten their fatigue on marches (Toro 1954). The Spanish, however, were so thorough in their destruction of the drug cults that these practices went underground for four centuries (Schultes 1960). Punished for their alleged superstitions, the Mexicans kept their sacred and magical plants hidden from the conquerors. After the conquest, Aztec culture declined, and today Nahuatl groups live in extreme poverty in refugee localities. We can no longer glean any vestige of their medicine or pharmacology from their present religious practices (del Pozo 1967). Gordon Wasson and his wife, however, upon a clue from the anthropologist Weitlander, discovered the use of sacred mushrooms in the hills of Oaxaca in the early 1950s, among isolated peasant peoples who used the plant to divine the future and seek a cure of illness (Wasson and Wasson 1957).

Sorcery and the Priesthood

Sacred plants were used most regularly by sorcerers and priests. by the time the Spanish arrived in the New World, Aztec religion contained a highly specialized priestly caste, numbering in the thousands, whose role was to interpret the designs and desires of the divinities. A group of priests called *calmecac* memorized traditions and history and acquired general knowledge. The priests used drugs like ololiuqui and the sacred mushrooms to administer to patients who sought their services for cures. Visual illusions were used to determine the cause of disease and the way to cure it (Schultes 1941). Sensory stimulation was very much part of the drug use, in that music, odors, and dances were part of ritual activity (del Pozo 1967). In addition to drug plants, the Aztecs had an impressive pharmacology of other plants and botanical gardens. Plants were given free of charge to patients as long as they returned and told the priests what the effects were for their particular illness. Aztec books existed which could be used by the priests as guides in healing illness or communicating with the supernatural.

The Aztec sorcerer was called a *ticitl*. Several Spanish priests have described his activities. It was believed that the sorcerer acquired his power through miraculous inspiration. For several days, he might go into a death-like trance. In many cases, the sorcerer's role was not malevolent; he was also considered to be a wise man, a doctor, and one who could divine the future and determine the cause of illness by using ololiuqui, tobacco, or peyote (Schultes 1941). If a person were sick, he would have to break the spell cast upon him by another. In this manner, ololiuqui was important in divining the cause of the illness. After drinking the potion containing this plant, a patient would relate his suspicions of bewitchment to the doctor (Schultes 1941).

The morning glory seeds often were ground up by priests into a potion and used in ointments to make a person fearless or to appease pain. The plant, in any form, was not taken in the midst of activities, but only in a secluded place. It was believed that drinking too much of an ololiuqui potion could lead to insanity. One early writer spoke of the use of peyote and ololiuqui by priests and magicians for their incantations (Acosta, cited in Brooks 1938). The plants were considered to be so holy that before starting on a journey to bring it back, the collectors were consecrated with incense. It was even considered a pious task to sweep the ground where ololiuqui grew (Safford 1916).

One incantation used to call upon the spirit of the powerful ololiuqui has been recorded for us by Jacinto de la Serna:

> Come now, come hither, Green Woman: behold the green
> heat (fever) and the brown heat: remove thou the flaming
> or scarlet heat, the yellow heat or by this token, I send
> thee to the seven caves. And I do command thee, put it
> not off till tomorrow or another day, for sooner or later
> thou wilt be compelled to do it. Who is the God—the so
> powerful and superior one—who can destroy the work of
> thy hands. It is I who command it, I the prince of
> enchantment. (cited in Safford 1916)

The seeds of ololiuqui were held in such reverence that candles were burned before them. They were stored in special boxes made for this purpose and sacrificial offerings were made to them in sacred niches in Aztec homes, despite unsuccessful Spanish attempts to erradicate this practice (Toro 1954).

Acosta, a Spanish prelate, found the use of these sacred plants distasteful, which may not be surprising considering that he wrote about Aztec priests who used an ointment made of venomous spiders, scorpions, salamanders, and vipers. This mixture was burned on the temple hearth and the ashes were mixed in mortars with tobacco. Ololiuqui was added to it, and the entire concoction was made into a drink. It was thought that it could deprive a man of his senses. It was also used as an offering to the gods, called "divine meat." By means of the ointment, Acosta wrote, "the priests lost all fear and became cruel in spirit. At night, they went alone into obscure caves and boasted that wild and savage beasts feared them because of the strength of their mixture" (cited in Schultes 1941). *Petun,* as this mixture was called (after the name of the tobacco plant used with it—a testimony to tobacco's place in the indigenous Mexican psychotropic pharmacopoeia) was used on occasion to heal the sick, and was called a divine physic. People came for all parts to the priests known for their skills in using the mixture. Another mixture of just tobacco and ololiuqui was known to numb the skin and was used as a plaster (ibid.).

Conclusions

Many of the psychotropic plants incorporated into ritual had a long history in Aztec society. From the barbarian tribes to the north, plants like peyote and divine mushrooms were used to enhance contact with supernatural realms. Such plants became widely diffused throughout the Valley of Mexico, and it was the Aztec who consolidated such use and eventually usurped such plants for priests, nobility, and special guests of the emperor. We know that the Aztec harshly punished drunkenness caused by alcohol, depending on the individual's status in society. Yet, inebriation caused by "divine messengers" seems to have received different treatment, no doubt because a clear distinction was made between fermented beverages and those plants that the Aztec believed permitted them access to preternatural realms, healed illness, and divined the future. As Aztec society became more and more stratified, such powerful plants were increasingly used by specialists for distinctive social goals, while the life of the laboring farmer remained one of sobriety and restraint.

Chapter 10

The Inca of Peru

The Inca, like the Aztecs, were recent arrivals to areas where ancient civilizations had previously flourished. Both the Inca and the Aztec barely had time to consolidate their newly won empires before the Spanish conquest. When we compare the two groups, we find that Inca society was much less mystically or philosophically oriented than the Maya or the Aztec. By this I mean that the achievements of the former centered around their great organizational skills in erecting one of the most cohesive and well-integrated theocratic empires in the history of humankind. The Aztec are distinguished by a legacy of philosophical treatises and astronomical knowledge. The Inca reached an urban level unsurpassed in human history, and they had a complex transportation system which joined their highland capital, Cuzco, to the entire Andean region. Harvests of simple farmers were controlled and redistributed; few people experienced hunger. It has been estimated that there were as many as ten million people in the empire.

Living by canal-irrigated terrace agriculture, with aqueducts and dikes for water control, the Inca took full advantage of guano manure from coastal islands, which they used to fertilize their lands, permitting them to accumulate and distribute large surpluses (Ribiero 1971). The Inca practiced mixed farming techniques and raised fur-bearing animals such as the llama and alpaca from whose coats they spun fine wool and wove some of the most elaborte textiles known to the world. Their populations were concentrated in cities of thousands of inhabitants, with fine temple and palace structures. The theocratic state was highly centralized, ruled by a hereditary nobility in the sacred person of the Inca, who was believed to be the son of the Sun. He was married to his sister. Other nobility administered the vast empire. Below the nobility in power was a lower-ranking stratum of priests, bureaucrats, and community headmen. An urban class of artists, physicians, architects, and artisans followed in power, and finally came the temporary conscripts to the Inca army, messengers, and soldiers. A vast clergy of priests and priestesses were devoted to the integration of the religious cult of Viracocha, the hero-civilizer, and the sun god, Pachacamac.

Relative newcomers on the Peruvian scene, the Inca were one of several militaristic local groups who brought diverse peoples under their domination. The conquered peoples in an area extending several thousand miles, from Ecuador to Chile, were made to speak Quechua. Unlike the Aztecs, however, the Inca came to use sacred plants late in their history and incorporated into their plant lists cultigens already in use by their conquered enemies. The Mochica civilization and the Chimu coastal civilization which followed it, for example, flourished from around the time of Christ to approximately A.D. 800, influencing much of Inca culture (see chapter 7 above and Lanning 1967), especially in their knowledge of sacred plants. At the level of the farmer, it is fairly certain that the San Pedro cactus played a continuous role in history right up to present times. For the Inca, the most important hallucinogens in addition to this cactus were the coca bush (*Erythroxylon coca*) and several varieties of Datura, as well as a hallucinogenic snuff (probably *Anadenanthera colubrina;* see Altshul 1972).

Coca

It has been estimated that the coca bush was cultivated some 2,000 years prior to the time that the Inca consolidated their empire. The first historical record that we have of its use was published some years after the Spanish murdered the last Inca ruler, Atahuallpa. The plant, from which the drug cocaine is extracted, includes over ninety species. The leaves were long used as a masticatory or chewing substance, and served as a medicine as well. Pharmacologically, cocaine has been listed legally as a controlled substance in the United States, although it would be most accurate to say that it is a stimulant, and not a narcotic, in its action on the central nervous system. The chewing of coca leaves, depending on quantity, can be quite similar in effect to the ingesting of cocaine. The leaves are generally chewed along with a ball of lime, which enhances the release of the alkaloid properties. Lime is obtained by burning the stalks of the *quinoa* plant, animal bones, sea shells, or limestone. Widely used among peoples of the Amazon Basin, coca was well established by the time that the Inca empire reached its peak in the Central Andes region (Martin 1970: 427).

Many coastal archaeological sites indicate the early use of coca. In the Nazca area to the south as well as along the north coast, pottery vessels show men with distended cheeks. Dried leaves, too, are found in many Peruvian mummy bundles dating back at least 2,000 years. Bags of leaves and lime pellets have been recorded. Coca leaves are represented in metallurgic art, in both gold and silver (Towle 1961). The Inca costume also included a bat, known as *chuspa*, to carry coca leaves. Coca was an emblem of the male children of the Inca, a sign of vigor and endurance (Perez de Barradas 1950: 22). Botanist R. T. Martin (1970) suggests that coca probably originated on the eastern slopes of the Andes Mountains of present-day Bolivia and Peru. Schultes (1960) argued that coca is a cultigen with a long association with human beings, since it is no longer known in the wild state. The most ancient use of coca probably was for shamanistic religious practices; it was valued for its ability to alleviate thirst and hunger. The mild mental excitation which follows the chewing of coca leaves may have permitted the shaman to enter with facility into a trance-like state so that he could communicate with the force of nature. It may be that this aspect of coca use—an enhancement of the trance-like state—is respon-

sible for its ancient name, "the divine plant." By the time of
Christ, Peruvian north coast pottery evidence shows scenes of
coca chewers. At that time, coca was probably used by persons
of high rank who were priests (Mortimer 1901).

As with Maya usurpation of plant hallucinogens, it is likely
that the Inca borrowed the use of coca, and with time, came to
consider it a most sacred plant. They believed it was a living
manifestation of divinity and treated its cultivation areas as sanc-
tuaries which inspired reverence from all people. The chronicler
Garcilaso de la Vega, who was the son of a Spanish captain and
an Inca noblewoman, recounted in his writings the Inca legend
about coca. It was said that the Children of the Sun presented
the Incas with the coca leaf to satisfy the hungry, to provide the
weary with new vigor, and to cause the unhappy to forget their
misery. Another legend explaining the origin of coca tells the
tale of Manco Capac, the wife of the fourth Inca, who was called
the "Mother of Coca." A beautiful woman who was killed because of her sexual excesses, her body was cut into pieces and
scattered on the ground. The coca bush was supposed to have
emerged from her remains, to give its rapturous leaves to human
beings (Mortimer 1901; Martin 1970).

The Inca restricted the use of coca largely to the nobility
and priests. Often, the Inca himself would reward his nobles
with gifts of coca. The chronicler José de Acosta wrote that during Inca times, common laborers could not use coca without a
license from the Inca or his governor. Young Inca noblemen, at
their initiation ceremonies, competed in foot races while young
women offered them coca and chica (the fermented corn drink)
to encourage fleetness of foot. As with the case of the Aztec use
of mushrooms, the nobles of conquered tribes who were to be
assimilated into the Empire were often given coca by the Inca
(Mortimer 1901).

Not only was coca used to facilitate trance states or reconcile
the grief of a community at conquest, but it was a vital adjunct
to court orators, who were specialists called *yaravecs*, men with
excellent memories able to relate the history of their people in
detail at royal council meetings. They were aided mainly by the
quipu, a mnemonic system of knotted strings. The yaravecs were

allowed to use coca, since it was believed that the plant strengthened their memory capacity (Martin 1970).

In the Inca capital of Cuzco, special sacrifices of coca were made. Supplicants approaching the altar were required to have coca in their mouths. During all Inca religious festivals, the leaves were thrown to the four cardinal points, or else burned on the altar. As with other hallucinogens, coca was used by the Inca to divine the future. The Inca consulted divine powers before undertaking most important activities, and he called upon coca to help make his decisions. Diviners would chew the leaves of the plant and spit the juice into their palms. They extended their two longest fingers and considered the augury thus viewed as favorable if the juice ran equally down both fingers, bad if it was unequal in its course. Another method of divining the future was to burn the leaves of the plant with the fat of the llama and watch the way it burned. The Inca maintained special plantations to grow the coca leaf, since it was so important to them in supernatural as well as medicinal activities (Martin 1970).

Storehouses containing coca could be found along the many Inca stone roads. These evenly paved thoroughfares led to the slopes and drying areas where coca was cultivated. The storehouses were used by both messengers and troops. It was said that the Inca himself, living in his capital city of Cuzco (which is two hours by jet plane today from the coastal city of Lima), could receive fresh fish for his dinner from a special relay messenger, called a *chasqui,* who carefully ran along engineered roads in two days' and nights' time. No doubt coca was a valuable asset to this messenger service for the endurance necessary to complete his task, which may have included warning others of events occurring in distant parts of the empire. Soldiers and messengers could endure incredibly long marches at high speeds by chewing coca. In the National Museum of Archaeology in Lima, there is a vase which depicts a wounded warrior who has a characteristic wad of coca bulging from his left cheek. The plant was not available, however, to the laboring farmer in the fields. Whatever plantations existed to raise coca were scarce and belonged exclusively to the Inca and his priests (Gamio 1937).

Gamio wrote that coca was used for both witchcraft and medicinal activities. A group of individuals called *inchuri* were believed to be witches and poisoners. Father Cobo, the Jesuit, wrote that they entered a sleeplike state to see the people they were curing. They interpreted their dreams and prepared potions of poisonous plants to kill people (probably their clients' enemies). They rubbed toads or guinea pigs over a sick person to extract his sickness symbolically. Coca was used by these witches to prevent magical emanations of divinities or occult forces. The Inca hated and feared such practitioners of black magic. Anyone believed guilty of murdering a person by black magic or poison would be killed, along with his entire family. This crime was one of the most heinous according to Inca law (Perez de Barradas 1950).

Coca was also offered to earth spirits. Local practitioners, who inherited their knowledge from other family members, were called *hampikatu*. They were skilled in the use of particular magical plants. Another group, called *callahuayas*, were itinerant travelers who went from town to town carrying diverse medicines. They helped to cure the sick and sold herbs, roots, and amulets to help people who believed that they were bewitched to overcome the bad luck that followed them. These travelers also divined the future. Their travels would take them from La Paz, Bolivia, north to Bogota, Colombia, and then south again to Argentina. They would often use coca to diagnose a person's illness; by allowing the leaves to fall upon the client, they would then interpret the way in which the patient was bewitched (Perez de Barradas 1950).

Coca apparently played an important role in facilitating digestion. The action of the plant enhances the assimilation of other foods, since it increases the flow of saliva and gastric secretions while strengthening gastro-intestinal muscles (Gutierrez-Noriega 1949). Since the food of the Quechua-speaking Indian consists largely of grains such as corn and barley, coca probably is as important today in the Indians' digestive process as it was in the past. Father Cobo (cited in Martin 1970) listed medicinal uses of the plant by indigenous doctors who used coca juice for treating stomach problems. They claimed that the plant would remove all gas and pains in the side. In decoction, it was regularly used as a laxative. Mixed with salt and egg white in small quantities, it was said to dry out and heal ulcers. Contemporary evidence concerning its beneficial effect on respiration gives us some insight into the plant's value during Inca times in high-altitude adaptation. Coca tea can bring quick relief from the alarming symptoms of *sorroche*, the mountain sickness characterized by nausea, dizziness, and headache which come from the low oxygen content of the air and the low atmospheric pressure. Cobo also described the use of coca in preventing illnesses of teeth and gums, and its use to make teeth white and strong. The plant was also employed to relieve the pains of rheumatism, headache, and external sores. In addition, coca has been reported by informants to be an aphrodisiac that restores lost vigor. The Inca goddess of love was represented as holding a leaf of coca in her hand. This was seen by some early writers to be a symbol of the reputed sexuality-enhancing virtues of the plant (Safford 1916).

A note is necessary here concerning the sumptuary use of coca by hieratic segments of the Inca empire. I am not suggesting that no coca use occurred at the folk level, once usurpation by state authorities occurred. Rather, one must be careful to distinguish between authority and power. The arguments presented here are based on the notion of legitimacy rather than a rule of "police state" enforcement. Moreover, as far as coca is concerned, we are probably not discussing a single stimulant, but conceivably a complex admixture of hallucinogens, stimulants, and alcohol.

The Spanish first observed the use of coca in 1533. It quickly spread to the masses and became an economically important plant to the Spanish in their exploitation of the New World raw materials. They gave coca to Indians who worked in mines and farmed in order to enable them to put in very long hours with little food or water. The Spanish enlarged existing coca plantations and sometimes paid off their Indian slave labor entirely in coca. In 1560, however, both political and ecclesiastic authorities set about to eradicate coca use on religious, medical, and humanitarian grounds, since they believed the plant was part of the Indians' idolatrous practices and was the creation of the devil as well (Blum 1969: 101).

Because of this pressure, the Crown issued edicts from time to time against the use of coca. From 1555 to 1561, Viceroy Canete attempted to suppress the Indians' use of coca at its very source—cultivation. Francisco de Toledo, the fifth viceroy, issued some seventy ordinances concerning coca. Nevertheless, these prohibitions failed, and coca became a monopoly first of the government and later of private entrepreneurs. It continued to be a currency for wages for near-slave laborers. The Indians themselves used it as money shortly after the conquest (Gamio 1937).

Much of highland folk medicine revolves around the use of the coca plant. In recent years, J. A. Gagliano has written an excellent summary article (1976) about the cultivation and consumption of coca in Peru, and Ernesto Mayer, a Peruvian anthropologist, has edited an authoritative volume in Spanish on the subject, entitled *Nuevas Perspectivas en Torno al Debate sobre el Uso de la Coca* (Anonymous 1978). The plant has aroused controversy since the beginnings of the Spanish conquest. After the sixteenth century, reports from the Andes ignored the significance of coca as a medicinal plant, focusing instead on its stimulative virtues or its value as a barter item. Some early reports did mention the Indians' use of the plant to obtain vigor and strength and to repress hunger and thirst.

Recent controversies developing over coca focus attention on the "miraculous" healing powers of the leaf and its use by native peoples for minor sicknesses such as nosebleeds, stomach disorders, and nausea (Hulshof 1978). Other authors, such as R. Bolton, and their adversaries argue over the role of coca in aggressive behavior of highland Ayamara and other Indian groups (see Bolton 1979; Bray and Dollery 1983).

In the highlands, the shamans employ coca as a remedy and instruct the client to mollify angry deities with various offerings, including coca leaves. In the seventeenth century, some healers were said to use coca "to conjure up the devil." By the eighteenth century, the leaf was regarded as an essential herb in the medical pharmacopoeias of the highland curandero. Even at this point, it was used for divination. During the nineteenth century, folk healers added Christian elements to their songs, evoking Christ and various saints. In divination rituals, the coca leaves would be scattered over a patient's shirt or poncho and the aid of a Christian saint would be solicited. The healer would blow on the leaves to determine the cause of illness, according to the direction in which the leaves accumulated. Mestizos believed that the leaf was a Satanic creation, and any healing powers attributed to it were diabolic illusions.

By the end of the sixteenth century, the plant entered into general medical use by white colonists in highland settlements. One writer, Paolo Mantegazza, wrote an article in 1859 (cited in Gagliano 1976) urging European scientists to investigate the medical potential of Peruvian coca, especially for use in dentistry. He wrote that the highland Indians also used the coca plant to treat hysteria and argued that it would be useful to experiment with coca in cases involving mental disorders such as melancholia, which in his opinion was less dangerous than using opium. He also wrote about coca's efficacy in ending caffeine addiction, since Peruvians had the habit of adding coca to their beverages instead of the caffeine they craved.

In recent years, the Peruvian government has tried to restrict coca cultivation by means of crop substitution. This endeavor has met with little success and has caused skepticism and controversy in many scientific circles. Sociologists and anthropologists argue that the use of coca has become so institutionalized in the popular medicine of the highland Indians that its eradication or even reduced consumption is unlikely.

Today, one does not find many coca chewers among lowlanders, except (until recently) among hacienda laborers who have migrated to coast areas from highland communities. In a recent article, however, Bray and Dollery (1983) argued that lowland coca chewing is much more widespread than has been generally acknowledged. Coca use is found universally throughout the Peruvian and Bolivian Andes, as well as through much of Colombia. As long as food, shelter, health, clothing, and fuel levels 402ain as they now are—abysmally poor—coca will no doubt continue to be used by native peoples of western South America. In many ways, the economies of these regions are intricately dependent upon the plant, whose use is so deeply rooted in the Andean region that the Indian way of life would have to undergo dramatic changes before coca use could be eliminated.

Other Mind-Altering Plants

Among the other plants that had important places in Inca life were a number of datura substances. It was believed that an influsion made from these powerful hallucinogens allowed Indian sorcerers to transport themselves into the presence of their ancestors and to work themselves into a state of ecstasy. Little is known about the use of datura seeds, but it is thought that they were used to produce delirium in order to discipline naughty children. One report suggests that datura was slipped into a cup of chicha as an aphrodisiac or as a love potion. Sometimes the plant might be put into fermented corn beer just to make it more intoxicating (Safford 1916: 404).

When the Spanish arrived in the New World, one of the datura group was given the name *yerba de Huaca*, or herb of a sacred shrine. In recent years, its trance-like effects have been used to gain clues as to the treasures concealed in shrines or ancient graves (Safford 1916: 404). When the medieval Spanish beliefs concerning grave-robbing and vampires were brought to the New World by superstitious Spanish soldiers, native plants like datura took on a new role.

Finally, a little-known hallucinogenic snuff called *wilka* or *huilca* (Anadenanthera peregrina) was used by the Inca. It has only been in recent years that more information has become available on this bush, whose seeds were also used in the chicha beverage as a purge. It was thought that sorcerers were able to communicate with their gods by the visions they had after mixing their beer with wilka seeds (Schultes 1960). Altschul, in an excellent monograph on the cultural use of the plant in American Indian societies, writes that amateur diviners and fortune-tellers spoke with the devil by drinking the juice of the seeds in tea, accompanied by ceremonies and sacrifices. Their diagnoses were made magically and secretly by their intoxication with the wilka juice (1972). Altschul argues from the cross-cultural evidence assembled in her monograph that wilka use in Inca civilization was primarily at the folk level and was not incorporated into hieratic religious activity. Nonetheless, its influence on the society must not be underestimated.

Conclusion

The Inca did not incorporate plant hallucinogens into their religious activities in nearly as elaborate a manner as their neighbors to the north. We can venture a guess that their pragmatic approach to life, as witnessed by their architectural and engineering feats, reflected relatively less interest in mind-altering plants than we find in other ancient civilizations whose environments were less challenging and whose philosophical and literary achievements were outstanding. The coca plant, in particular, seems to have been used by the Inca in a variety of ways to aid individuals in pragmatic goals, such as obtaining the greatest performance out of many of the messenger groups, or else as a reward for special activity. Plant hallucinogens served, to a lesser extent than did some plants in other cultures, as a bridge to the supernatural to aid in diagnosing and treating illness.

Chapter 11

The Fang of Northwestern Equatorial Africa

In the northwestern portion of equatorial Africa, a tribal group known as the Fang inhabit an area of Zaire with high temperature and humidity, heavy rainfall, and dense forests. Living in distinct villages, the Fang farm peanuts, corn, manioc, and plantains. An agricultural and commerce-oriented people, the Fang have experienced the shock of European colonialism for the last hundred years. With the coming of the French, many of their aboriginal life patterns changed. In fact, a new culture emerged as the result of forced borrowing. Some anthropologists, like George Balandier (1963), suggest that the resultant amalgamation, with the advent of a colonial money economy and the alienation of the peasantry from the land, has caused social disequilibrium.

The Fang use the hallucinogenic plant *Tabernanthe iboga* (fig. 28) in a number of interesting ways. In the past, during precontact times, the plant was taken to relieve fatigue and to aid in hunting. Today, however, this hallucinogen receives its greatest elaboration in response to the disorienting changes that have occurred in the wake of culture contact. In particular, the Tabernanthe iboga bush has been incorporated into a religious revitalization movement known as the *Bwiti*, which can be dated to the end of the last century. It appeared in full force about the

Figure 28. Tabernanthe iboga. (*After Stafford 1977: 322*)

time of the First World War (Fernandez 1972). Our knowledge of Bwiti goes back to secret societies in French West Africa which appeared as early as 1863 (de Veciana 1958).

Prior to its incorporation in the Bwiti cult, the plant gained a reputation in Europe as a powerful stimulant and aphrodisiac, surpassing even the renowned *Yohimbine* plant for its alleged sexual benefits (Pope 1969). There is no pharmacologic evidence that the alkaloid ibogaine directly stimulates sexual functions; some authors, nonetheless, maintain that it increases an individual's confidence and removes fatigue, which perhaps accounts for its fame. Several reports have appeared in scattered sources about the use of the plant by warriors and hunters who found it an excellent way to keep themselves constantly awake during night watches or while hunting for game.

Three important alkaloids have been isolated from among twelve others in the plant. They are somewhat comparable to cocaine, but they possess definite hallucinatory properties. They are Tabernatheine, Ibogamine, and Iboluteine, described in 1953 by Goutarel and Janot (Balandier 1963). In addition, three other plant hallucinogens are used in cultic activity, but Iboga is the most important (Fernandez 1972). The plant is a member of the Apocynacea family and is found mainly in Gabon, although it is used in the adjacent regions of Zaire, Angola, and as far north as the Cameroons. The shrub is about three or four feet in height and grows wild. It is also cultivated around native huts. Large dosages bring on fantastic visions, convulsions, and paralysis as well as an occasional death. The effects of large dosages have been reported by a Belgian, Guien, who observed its use in Zaire. Describing an initiate's experience in the Bwiti movement, Guien wrote: "Soon all his sinews stretched out in an extraordinary fashion. An epileptic madness seizes him during which, unconscious, he mouths words which when heard by the initiated have a prophetic meaning and prove that the fetish has entered him" (1903, cited in Pope 1969). Gabonese informants reported to botanists studying the plant that it was identical to alcohol, although it did not disturb thought processes. Small amounts of iboga produce marginal hallucinatory effects, possibly a dreamy or floating sensation (ibid.).

Only some 10 percent of the Fang people are involved in the minority movement called Bwiti. The frustrations of the colonial situation that Balandier sees as the catalytic agent make the Bwiti movement very much like the peyote cult found among North American Indians. The Bwiti cult most probably originated among the Mitsogo or Apindji peoples of Central Gabon, in an area where iboga is most abundant. Many rituals and beliefs of adjacent Bantu peoples were borrowed and incorporated into the cult. By 1923, many tribal groups in the area used the plant in religious activities, including the Baloumbo, Bayaka, Issoga, and Ashango. In 1924, Danay published an article on some indigenous peoples of Gabon, in which he stressed the importance of Bwiti as an intercessor between man and an immortal god called Mwanga (cited in de Veciana 1958). In recent years, two anthropologists, Balandier (1957, 1963) and Fernandez (1965, 1972, 1982), have both studied the use of iboga among the Fang.

One early report, dating from 1897, stated that the hallucinatory properties of the plant were revealed to Gabon blacks by the Pygmies (Fernandez 1972; Pope 1969), who learned that by chewing the plant, one could pass various days and nights without sleeping and one could see forms which could be extraordinarily terrible or wonderful. Some reports attributed the use of the plant to boars, porcupines, and gorillas. In particular, boars were thought to dig up and eat the roots of the plant, only to go into a wild frenzy, jumping around in fright from their visions (Pope 1969).

Initiation into the Bwiti cult comes about when one sees the Bwiti by eating the iboga. "The Bwiti" is used to refer to both a superior divinity who is revealed to the initiate and a sculpture post which constitutes the fundamental temple symbol. The term also refers to the ancestors and the supernatural realm of the dead, as well as the great gods of the Christian hierarchy (Fernandez 1972). The plant constitutes the distinctive mark of the members of the movement, and has a considerable place in it. Men who drink the iboga make a preparation from the gratings of the plant or sometimes eat the plant directly (Pope 1969).

The movement numbers men among its principal members, although Mbiri, a sister sect, includes women (Fernandez 1972). Bwiti grew prodigiously from 1920 to 1930, spreading across the Cameroons and the Amban region. There was official French colonial and missionary opposition to Bwiti: in 1931, some temples were actually destroyed, which caused the group's activities to become clandestine. As a result, after the Second World War, Bwiti villages tended to concentrate in marginal areas. Balandier viewed the cult as syncretic in nature (1963), blending elements of traditional Fang beliefs with Christian symbols. Today the cult operates to honor particular ancestors, to conduct rites linked to fertility, and, in effect, to help cement feelings of cohesion and solidarity. Those villages where the Bwiti movement is established have a temple that occupies a position of privilege in the village, generally found near the central street; members live nearby (Balandier 1963). In past times, it was necessary to make a human sacrifice in order to found a new temple, but today the human victim has been replaced by a chicken. The sacrifice symbolizes breaking with kinship and normal social ties, prior to the establishment of new ones in the movement.

Each temple has a central post covered with carved figures and symbols which express the personality, so to speak, of different groups. Balandier (1963) has distinguished three types of post symbolism in cult worship. The first is rudimentary: the post generally contains female sexual motifs. A second type has more intricate sculpture of women with the genitalia and breasts precisely rendered. Balandier argues that this second type of carving represents the principal female divinity, the first woman, who is a link between the earth and the sky. The third type of post has rich and composite symbolism incorporating various Christian features. These three types of iconography correlate well from the least to the most acculturated villages, where Western ways and elements of Christianity have taken greatest root. Temples tend to be quite large and impressive. Symbolic representations include birds of death, which sing only at night to keep death away from a person who is listening. Other iconic representations include the thunder symbol, various animals, and so on. Toward the interior part of the temple, one finds

symbols of the earth, star, night and day, life, windows of the
world, and crosses. Along the sides, a python serpent is represented, corresponding to a rainbow, which plays an important
role in the movement. Defenses against evil directed toward the
Bwiti society are common. Balandier views the cult as presenting
its members with a cosmogony of religious thoughts centered
on the idea of fecundity and death, as well as a defense against
the dangers of sorcery. This latter phenomenon has increased
tremendously in recent decades because of social disorganization. With conflict and individual competition the mark of changing social conditions, Bwiti members view this defense as very
important.

In the center of the temple there is a sanctuary lamp. A harp
and an impromptu drum are used to provide music and rhythmic
beating. Music plays an important role in Bwiti, as Fernandez
reports (1972). Balandier points out the important dualism found
in the Bwiti beliefs, such as masculine and feminine, night and
day, heaven and earth, birth and death, good and evil, and so
forth (see also Fernandez 1972). As we noted with regard to the
Maya, these dual concepts may be related to the polarities of
feeling—the anguish or euphoria—experienced in the wake of
hallucinogenic plant use. Generally, of course, dualities are part
of most religious systems.

The iboga is generally consumed first by Bwiti members at
their initiation, after they have painted their bodies white and
red, symbols of good and evil. Parrot feathers are also used as
adornment. When initiates in some areas take the iboga plant,
they are dressed in tiger skins, which are part of the warrior's
traditional costume. Ornamental designs are painted on their
faces and bodies, and a headdress of feathers is placed in their
hair. Under the influence of the plant, they appreciate deeply
such resplendent costumes, which probably help to stimulate
the perceptual distortions brought on by the plant. It is believed
that the plant offers revelations and power to the new member.
He is admitted to the inner circle of the sect, called Akum, solely
on the quality of his revelation. The candidate is involved closely
with his hallucinatory visions for several days. The Fang highly
value revealed knowledge, which they see as a separate reality

from that of everyday life. It is only revealed knowledge that permits a particular commitment and carries the appropriate qualification for an individual to enter the cult: the initiate must see the divinity of the Bwiti himself. Balandier (1963) calls this culturally valued vision "stereotyped." Thus the expectation of seeing the Bwiti divinity structures the nature of a given subjective hallucinogenic experience, so that most, if not all, candidates claim to see this power, real or imagined. In addition to the Bwiti spirit, the candidate directly communicates with an assembly of dead ones, a chain of ancestors.

One report describes a Bwiti vision that features a small human form the color of fire, which appears before the Akum member's eye in a grotesque dance. Balandier believes that the Bwiti symbols may be related to a cult of fire (1963). The initiate falls to the ground in a stupor after drinking the iboga. During this period of lethargy, the Bwiti is supposed to reveal itself under the most diverse and macabre forms. The sleeping man will see a phantasm arrive, which takes him by the hand and conducts him around one thousand turns and detours to a place which has only one hut and one door. This phantasm-guide opens the door; then the initiate sees a long procession of skeletons and cadavers pass in front of his eyes, pale, gesticulating, and giving off an insufferable odor. The chief of this "city of the dead," an individual even more repulsive than the others, asks the candidate: "What are you doing here?" He replies, "I come to see Bwiti." The vision answers, "That is I," and the vision disappears. During this strange sleep, the man sometimes cries out in terror or uses unintelligible words, but others are sure at this moment that he is in communication with Bwiti. When the candidate returns to his normal state, he is interrogated by the initiated men, to see if his vision is sufficiently appropriate so that he can be admitted. Generally this happens. As one commentator has written, should the individual not see the Bwiti, he is given repeated doses of iboga, a procedure which probably kills both him and his doubts (Balandier 1963). Fernandez reports some dozen cases in the last forty years where initiates have died from suspected overdoses (1972).

Somatic discomfort present in the actual hallucinogenic experience can take on the visual apparitions often reported in the forms of cadavers, skeletons, or funny-looking creatures with large, bony feet. Such visionary experience is valued by the Fang, whose traditional cultural focus has been to worship ancestors, who play an important role in directing the lives of those still on earth.

In his fieldwork, Fernandez obtained reports concerning stereotypic drug visions. In a sample of fifty people, 40 percent saw dead relatives who instructed them to eat iboga; another 24 percent were counseled to eat iboga to cure an illness. An important stereotypic vision showed the initiate walking over a long multicolored road or over many rivers leading to one's ancestors, who then took the initiate to the great gods. Fernandez relates this to the importance that the Fang attach to their genealogies, which reaffirm man's relationship to his ancestors. This importance explains the columns of dead people in iboga visions, which Fernandez sees as legendary genealogical frameworks. As Fernandez argues, the Fang took iboga because of a need to see, to know, and to communicate with greater powers hidden in and known through the plant (1972, 1982).

Balandier (1963) wrote that the Bwiti movement indicates to us how very much the traditional religious experience of the Fang has not changed despite long periods of Christian proselytism. Thus Bwiti is seen as a living religion, true to life, while Christianity is acquired, learned, but not felt or experienced through ecstatic revelation. However, many of the Bwiti myths show clear Christian influence in cosmogony and culture heroes. For example, an equivalence seems to have been reached between the Virgin Mary and the cult's First Woman. This is syncretized with rites where ancient names in initiation rites coincide with the name of each person's animal protector.

One of the major goals of the movement members, as described by Fernandez, is to achieve a state of one-heartedness, after night-long rituals during which they consume iboga. The ritual, recurring various times a month, relies upon moderate amounts of iboga to achieve ecstatic states. Fernandez states that Bwiti cult members do not look kindly on heavy ingestion of iboga by members, except during initiation when they are engaged in the search for deep contacts with Bwiti (1972). Informants told Fernandez that the plant was taken to make the body light and to enable the soul to fly. Dancing before midnight celebrates creation, birth, and migration from the land of the dead. Dancing after midnight represents death and the return to the land of the dead. Christianity has taught the Fang the idea that punishment after death follows one's earthly life, so they have modified traditional African concepts which state that their ancestors can intervene in favor of the living.

One ritual described by Swiderski (1965) is interesting to read:

> On the day of the initiation, the candidates go to the "temple of the universe" accompanied by their fathers and maternal uncle at 6:00 in the morning. There, they are given two shallow baskets, each about eight inches in diameter, filled with raspings of the iboga root. The priest stands in front of the boys and says, "See this stuff at your feet which you must like, even though it tastes as repugnant as heavy oil. If I give it to you will you consume it?" The boys reply: "Give and I will consume it gladly." The priest responds: "Take it then, but with the mouth and not the hands."

While the priest and family watch, the boys devour the bitter, vile-tasting cuttings. Throughout the day, they eat the iboga continually, but it isn't until later that day that the candidates have eaten enough iboga to see the Bwiti. The evening ceremonies begin with a ritual dance by all members of the Bwiti cult. At the end of the dance, the boys go off to a specially prepared hut where they continue to eat iboga, and then dance vigorously afterward. Toward nightfall, the *lomba,* or central part of the ceremony, begins. A sorcerer dances about two hours, and invokes the ancestors of the members. Then there is a torch-light dance, during which time iboga seems to cause its peak effects in the individual imbibers. They fall silent while the sacred harp melody is played. One by one, the candidates murmur as they begin to see the Bwiti. Visions continue several hours, and then the initiates fall into a sleep that can last for five to seven days. Fernandez (1965) points out that this pattern can vary:

among the Asumege Ening branch, the initiate at times is sent into the forest for several days after eating the iboga. Other tribal groups may add other plants, especially one considered to be an aphrodisiac. At times, concoctions can contain as many as ten plant varieties.

The sacred iboga plant is used several times during the life of the Bwiti cult member. Sorcerers take a drink of it before demanding information from the spirits. The leaders of the cult eat iboga for an entire day before asking their ancestors to give them advice. In many ways, the Bwiti has preserved part of the Fang cultural heritage. As with American peyotists, Bwiti members have crystalized tribal features. Sect cohesion is reinforced by the sentiment of the members, who believe that they have superior knowledge. The initiated candidate is told of the great honor he is receiving by knowing about the things of the earth; he is bound by sacred rules enforced under penalty of death. There is a certain quality of clandestinity involved in becoming a Bwiti member. Periodic sacrifices are held, and all the members participate in public ceremonies. Most festivities are linked to initiation rites, which place the sect in the center of all village or intervillage activities. In the past, active opposition of missionaries and colonial administrators helped the movement achieve cohesion. It is a religion which has reference not only to one's immediate clan ancestors but to all the ancestors of the community. A hierarchy has been established between different Bwiti centers and zones of influence. These ritual centers reinforce the unity of Fang symbolic representations, myths, rituals, and dances, and reconfirm the authority of a priest who oversees initiations and acts as a guide during the drug session. To some degree, the movement operates to efface antagonisms of ethnic or clan conflict.

Bwiti is viewed by Balandier (1963) as establishing a certain order in a society where ancient systems of social control have become eroded and where colonial conditions are dehumanizing. There is a real need to reintegrate individuals who have been alienated over long periods of time from their traditional kinship ties. The fragmentation and atomization so commonplace in advanced industrial society has left traditional groups without any anchor. The Bwiti give these kinship groups a sanctified character by using the iboga plant, especially since it permits direct communication with the valued ghosts of the past. Benefits include the focus on the strength the individual is believed to obtain from using the plant and the assurances of fertility which people believe they derive from their membership in the cult. In addition, several of Balandier's informants spoke of their desire to obtain knowledge of things of the other world, which the hallucinogen made available to them. Moreover, Bwiti members see in the plant the possibility of compensating for their social inferiority in the face of the European intrusion into their society of superior material wealth and power. Thus, for the Fang, the hallucinatory substance helps people adapt from a state of social instability to one of cohesive well-being. By the quality of the knowledge they are able to obtain in the drug experience, Bwiti cult members receive an orientation and a point of reference in their search for security.

Chapter 12

Urban Amazonian Mestizos of Peru

In the tropical rain forest of Peru, Colombia, and Brazil, called the montaña, a woody vine, ayahuasca, is used by tribal horticultural groups and urbanized Mestizo populations as an integral part of folk healing (Lemlij 1965). Comprising various species of *Banisteriopsis*, whose principal alkaloids harmine, harmaline, and tetrohydroharmaline are responsible for the psychoactive effects reported, ayahuasca is as powerful as LSD but much less generally known.

Especially in the Peruvian Amazon region this hallucinogenic substance has found particular elaboration in folk psychiatry in healing illnesses that are mainly emotional or psychological in origin. Folk healers, called *ayahuasqueros*, assemble groups of patients several times a week in isolated jungle clearings near urban centers, where they use a drink prepared from ayahuasca in ritual curing.

Ayahuasca is used not only by city dwellers but also by jungle farmers in scattered river hamlets and members of fast-disappearing primitive groups. Folk healing practices in urban jungle areas, including the Amazon city of Iquitos (located some 2,300 miles inland, west of the Atlantic Ocean), represent a complex amalgam of traditional healing practices and twentieth-century medical science. The kind of urban drug-adjuncted heal-

Figure 29. Banisteriopsis caapi. (*After Stafford 1977: 257*)

ing discussed in this chapter must be viewed also as a complex interweaving of tribal Indian beliefs with a minimal admixture of Mestizo Roman Catholic religious ideology. Illness has a magical causality for both urban poor and middle-class individuals. They call upon this belief system to explain the ubiquitous problems posed by the threat of disease, infirmity, and misfortune.

I gathered the data for this chapter during a year's field investigation in Peru in 1968–69. In Belen, an urban slum in Iquitos, I gathered beliefs about illness and followed patients as they visited ayahuasca healers (see Dobkin de Rios 1972a). As in many other parts of the world undergoing rapid social change, folk healers here tend to have the greatest amount of success in the treatment of socially and emotionally precipitated illness (Kleinman and Sung 1979). Psychosomatic disorders provide ayahuasca healers with their largest single group of illnesses, although most folk healers are skilled in recognizing and treating simple afflictions such as colds, fevers, skin disorders, and the like.

I will begin by discussing the history of ayahuasca use among tribal horticultural groups and analyzing the use of the substance in urban curing, particularly the ceremonial and ritual uses. Cultural etiology of disease and culturally standardized visions utilized by the healers are also important. Cultural variables in drug-adjuncted healing must be seen as central in order to understand how cultural expectations can shape subjective visual imagery.

Traditional Uses of Ayahuasca

The main area in which ayahuasca is used is the confluence of the Upper Orinoco and Amazon rivers, where Cooper (1949) reported many Indian groups using *Banisteriopsis* for exciting and pleasurable effects. Ayahuasca has been used in tribal societies:

1. to learn the whereabouts of enemies and to discover their plans (Villavicencio 1858; Spruce 1908);
2. before going off to war, to hunt, or on other expeditions (Reinburg 1921);

3. as an aid in acquiring a special protective spirit (Harner 1962);
4. in association with tribal religious beliefs (Cooper 1949; Karsten 1923; Schultes 1957; Spruce 1908);
5. to give answers to emissaries of other groups (Spruce 1908);
6. to tell if strangers were coming (Spruce 1908);
7. to tell if wives were unfaithful (Spruce 1908);
8. to prophesy the future clearly (Reinburg 1921; Roessner 1946; Schultes 1957);
9. for pleasurable or aphrodisiacal effects (Reinburg 1921; Wiffen 1915); and
10. for use in determining the cause and effecting a cure of disease (Barret 1932; Harner 1968; Karsten 1923; Koch-Grunberg 1908; Perez de Barradas 1950; Reinburg 1921; Spruce 1908; Wiffen 1915).

A study by Siskind (1973) among the Sharanahua Indians of the Peru-Brazil border illustrates the centrality of ayahuasca to all healing in the community. One shaman observed by Siskind in a community of 80 people used the plant in 27 cases in a year. Needless to say, then, in the above list of ways in which the plant was used, Western categories that separate healing from religion are spurious, especially when taboo violation, the malevolent spirits of nature, or the evil malice of others may be deemed responsible for the cause of illness within a given social context.

Background Data

Peruvian tropical rain forest cities such as Iquitos, where ayahuasca healing is commonplace, are relatively new urban areas. Penetration of the jungle region by the Peruvian nation-state was difficult because of the inaccessibility of the vast tracts of land that lay to the east of the high Andean mountains. Nonetheless, the jungle was explored in the sixteenth century by Spanish conquistadores lured by tales of the fabulous land of El Dorado, which they believed lay toward the east. Various expeditions set out from the coast to find this mythical land of

riches, to no avail. Jesuit, Franciscan, and Augustine missionaries followed shortly thereafter. It was only Portuguese expan-
sion in the mid nineteenth century that motivated the Peruvian
government to consolidate the large tracts of rain forest that, at
least in name, were part of the national territory. The rubber
boom in the late part of the nineteenth century brought about
the rapid growth of Iquitos, which was officially founded in 1860.
Hordes of migrants, both from the jungle and abroad, came to
cities like Iquitos and Pucallpa.

Today Iquitos appears to be a modern city. Yet despite the
city's cement splendor, so different from the thatched wooden
huts found in jungle hamlets, highly developed hallucinogenic
healing rituals are found in both the city and the hamlets. Traditional belief systems concerning illness and healing have sur-
vived the shock of acculturative forces to become firmly entrenched
in twentieth-century urban life. Both ayahuasca patients and
healers are drawn in large numbers from the thousands of people
who live in Iquitos. Middle-class merchants, their families, army
personnel, government employees, artisans, and laborers who
reside in far-spread neighborhoods in Iquitos fill the consultation
rooms of the ayahuasca healers or come to their jungle healing
sessions. Belief in the efficacy of the drug healer and his powerful
vine pervade all segments of the society. Well-dressed merchants
and professional men as well as recent immigrants seek in the
powerful purge, as the plant emetic is called, a last resort in
their attempt to be cured. It is in Belen, an urban slum located
at the foot of Iquitos, that continuity with the rest of jungle life
can be most clearly observed. Belen serves as a port of entry
both for jungle produce and for migrants seeking work and
better schools for their children.

Healing Sessions

Two or three nights a week, at about 10:00 P.M., an ayahuasquero assembles his patients, preferably in a jungle clearing
at the edge of the city. Settling comfortably in a circle on plastic
mats both the hearler and his patients drink a potion prepared
by boiling the woody vine several hours, often with such ad-

ditives as *toé* (*Datura speciosa*) or *chacruna* (*Banisteriopsis rusbyana*, containing DMT). At times, a narcotic tobacco may be taken somewhat later in the session (identified as *Nicotiana tabacum*). Special whistling incantations accompany the communal cup of ayahuasca passed around the circle by the healer. Each patient receives an amount varied in accordance with several factors: body weight, the nature of his illness (is it chronic or not?), and his general state of health. In some cases, a healer may prepare a special liquid for a particular patient.

About 20 minutes to half an hour later, when the psychoactive effects of the drink are being experienced—altered visual perception, greater sensitivity to sound, feelings of depersonalization or the sense of leaving one's body, synesthesia, and so on—the healer will begin a continuing series of songs and whistles that are believed important in regulating and evoking peoples' visions. Because the purge frequently causes nausea, vomiting, and occasional diarrhea in initial experiences, the early part of a healing session may include people spitting out the bitter taste of the liquid or vomiting off to one side. None of these noises are kept from the rest of the group. As the evening progresses, the healer moves around the circle contacting each person, accompanied by his ever-present *schacapa* rattle, made from the dried leaves of a jungle plant tied together with a vine to give off a rustling, rattling noise. During the curing ceremony, the healer will blow tobacco smoke (called in Spanish, *mapacho*) over the body of an afflicted person. If a patient experiences pain in a particular part of his body, a healer may suck the dolorous area and bring forth a spine or thistle, which everyone present is apt to believe was magically introduced by an enemy or evil spirit. Each patient receives counseling and is ritually exorcised by the healer during the course of the session. Finally, at two or three in the morning, after some four or five hours of strong drug intoxication, the patient may return to his home, or spend the night in a thatched, wall-less jungle shelter which is often near the spot where the session is held. Dietary proscriptions form a part of ayahuasca healing, as it is believed that the vine has a jealous guardian spirit. For this reason, patients abstain from salt, lard, and sweets for at least 24 hours preceding and following the use of the purge. In addition, special diets may be prescribed by healers for particular patients.

Ayahuasqueros not only use the powerful vine in healing, but are quite knowledgeable about the vast number of pharmaceutical medicines on the market, and they prescribe them for some of their clients, as well as a host of plants and herbs which they themselves prepare as remedies for particular illnesses. The psychoactive ayahuasca drink is used mainly to diagnose the magical causality of illness, as well as to deflect and neutralize the evil magic that is deemed responsible for certain types of illness. In no way does the drug serve as a panacea for sickness; rather it is part of a complex ritual healing ceremony. It is important to examine the nexus of social relations in which this hallucinogenic healing takes place in order to comprehend better the particular place that ayahuasca has in ritual.

Methodology

I conducted fieldwork in the urban slum or *barriada* of Belen, where a base ethnography was established both through my participant observation and by means of analysis of data available from a series of sociological surveys that had been conducted a few years earlier by one of the governmental agencies and the local university (see Wils 1966; Oviedo 1964). I gathered data on belief systems concerning illness and cultural etiology of disease by means of interviews with a representative number of healers and patients, and attended several healing sessions in the company of patients' informants; as a friend or companion, I was called upon to help people home after difficult moments of drug intoxication (a cultural role that already existed). In addition, I took 100 micrograms of LSD, and later attended an ayahuasca sessions during which I drank a potion containing ayahuasca and chacruna. I believe that a drug researcher must have some subjective experience in order to understand the nature of informants' reports. This was particularly applicable in the ayahuasca study, as notebooks full of culturally reported visions seemed difficult to comprehend until my own subjective experience clarified the veracity of reports about seeing unidentified persons "appear in living color" and so on. In addition, recounting my own experience with ayahuasca provided me an excellent means of entry into the world of personal experience among informants, who were more likely to discuss their own visions with another person who had also participated. My participant observation experiences were most helpful in establishing rapport.

The Structure of a Slum

Belen is situated on the Amazon River, at the foot of the city of Iquitos, which is set upon an eroding palisade some 200 meters above sea level and is literally an island in the jungle. Each year, tropical rain-forest lands adjoining the community give way to urban growth as population grows. No major roads connect the city with other areas. The river serves as the major artery of communication apart from daily air service to the national capital, Lima, or other jungle or highland cities.

Belen is an excellent area in which to gather data on jungle beliefs that come into head-on collision with city life. Although scattered jungle hamlets, consisting of anywhere from 25 to several hundred families, can be studied in terms of similar structural characteristics, slum life—with exceedingly high unemployment rates, excessive malnutrition, family breakdown, prostitution, vandalism, chronic illness, and a host of other social pathologies—sets the stage for a much more intense kind of social analysis than that available in many community studies. Other urban slum analyses have focused upon networks of interacting dyadic relationships, pointing out that structures do exist within the seemingly amorphous community. In an area like Belen, the fieldworker finds herself knowing people who do not know their neighbors and have little, if any, shared community tradition. Even the "amoral familiarism" that Banfield (1958) describes in South Italian communities does not enter into the picture, as family unions here are fragile and relationships between the sexes are filled with tension and explosive to observe. I have explored elsewhere data on elaborate systems of love magic prominent in the community, in an attempt to relate such beliefs to the harsh economic facts of life (see Dobkin de Rios 1969). Fortunately, because of the various sociological surveys that carpeted this community, a large data base is available for analysis. Participant observation brings forth qualitative aspects of social life where illness haunts the footsteps of most people (see Kellert et al. 1967).

No doubt because of the extreme economic insecurity owing to lack of jobs and the unavailability of jungle lands for farming, men and women work mainly at commercial activity tied to the movement of forest produce to the city markets located on the palisade above the slum community. Small-scale wholesaling of such produce, with little capital, is common, as vegetables, fish, and other jungle resources are resold again at the city market for a small profit. *Rematistas*, as these wholesalers are called, constitute the largest single occupational category in Belen. Others, more favored with accumulated capital, own motor-powered boats which they load with staples such as rice, sugar, coffee, and gasoline. These entrepreneurs, called *regatones*, ply the many river inlets and sell their staples at a considerable mark-up to one-crop river hamlet residents. Jungle peasants devote much of their time to such activities as hunting precious animal pelts, which they sell to merchants in Iquitos. These pelts, in turn, are sold to luxury stores in Europe or North America at thousands of percentage profit. Hunters carry pelts long distances to docked boats, leaving protein-rich meat to rot in the jungle. Others work at tropical fish extraction, which brings a small cash income, and become needy buyers of the food staples that the regatones bring on their monthly calls.

Belen is quite unlike the jungle hamelts from which most migrants came, since farm land is not available and people live crowded together in an area that is flooded at least four months a year. During this time, houses must be abandoned, or, if they are built on balsa log supports or on an actual balsa raft, they rise with the water level, leaving householders to use canoes to get around or pay children to ferry them to market. Fishermen used to be able to work close by home in the waters of the nearby Itaya River, but with growing population and indiscriminate fishing, natural resources have been fast disappearing and fishing trips take men away from Belen for periods of up to four to six weeks. Women and children get left behind, staying alive as best they can by reselling produce in the market, or from the money their children earn at odd jobs to help them out. Unlike other urban slums throughout Latin America, male outmigration is a relatively minor phenomenon, and fewer than 30 percent of the population at the time of the study left the community. Other jungle areas, too, are economically depressed, so jobs are not easily available elsewhere. Lima, the national capital, is far away and costly to reach.

Everyday life of the people of Belen is marked by immense overcrowding, inadequate health conditions, high parasitosis, and high levels of malnutrition. Disease is a constant companion. Many different types of illness are commonly delineated, some of which are simple and believed to come from God. Colds, upper-respiratory infections, fevers, and the like easily respond to medication and rest; poorly trained medical aides, called *sanitorios*, are frequent slum visitors who dispense penicillin or antibiotic injections for a small fee. Formal medical consultation in the city above is far too costly for most slum residents, and the city hospital has the reputation as a place one goes to die, especially for its casual way of dealing with poor people.

If a simple fever, pain, or ache does not respond well to an injection, tonic, or medicine, however, many Belen residents conclude that their illness may originate from the malice of another, or from punishment from some natural spirit. Perhaps one has broken some taboo which has offended a spirit of nature. For example, a menstruating woman who bathes before three days have passed may hemorrhage because of the punishment of the offended spirit. Although much jungle illness is attributed to taboo violation, case histories collected in Belen frequently focus upon evil willing on the part of others who were deemed responsible for sickness or misfortune. In this second category of magical illness, bewitchment by means of consulting with a powerful witch is often viewed as the cause of illness. Others may be feared because they place a powerful potion in a drink to cause the individual harm. People claim they know when they have been bewitched by the suddenness of the onset of aches and pains in a particular part of their body.

As in many parts of the world where beliefs in magic, witch-craft, and sorcery are handmaidens to modern medicine, one finds that people seek different sets of answers to eternal problems of illness. How one's body has been attacked by micro-organisms and how illness spreads through it is not of much interest in a world where causal factors are viewed primarily within a magical framework. Thus, the "why me?" and not the "how?" is the subject of inquiry into disease and all its ramifications. A person's concern upon entering a world of impaired functioning is to find out exactly why he and not someone else is afflicted by disease. Nor are the answers simple ones, especially in the light of ongoing culture change where twentieth-century medical science has made certain inroads.

The particular categories of magical illness that I will describe shortly afflict patients whose anxieties, fears, and projections of hostility and hatred toward others would, in Western medicine, be cause for psychiatric help. Drug healing in the Peruvian jungle in many ways represents a very old and time-honored tradition of dealing with psychological problems—one that predates Freudian analysis by many centuries.

Magical Illnesses and Their Causes

Several major illnesses caused by the willing of evil by others are recognized by most Belen residents. Once I established rapport with informants, they poured out confidences in rapid succession about the malice to be found in the hearts of their neighbors or relatives, who often seek out a *brujo* (witch) to cause someone harm. Most ayahuasqueros refuse this trade, but others are willing and specialize in the use of psychoactive drugs for socially defined evil purposes. They maintain that while intoxicated by the drug, they can leave their bodies and inflict harm—even incurable disease—upon their clients' enemies.

The following categories of magical illness were elicited from informants in Belen.

SUSTO   A common illness found throughout Peru and Latin America, this infirmity includes cases of profound alteration of metabolism, or nervous disorder. *Susto* is an intense psychic trauma provoked by an emotion of fear, and its symptoms include lack of appetite and energy. The disease is caused by the "loss of the sick person's soul." It is one of the types of illness treated most frequently by Peruvian folk healers (see Sal y Rosas 1958).

DAÑO   People say that they suffer from *daño* because they are envied by others (*envidia*) or because someone harbors feelings of vengeance toward them (*despecho*). Beleños recognize the important role that interpersonal strife and stress can play in generating such infirmities. Daño can be associated with a large number of illnesses including hemorrhaging, muscular pain, loss of consciousness, suffocation, tumors, and consistent bad luck (called *saladera*). What is crucial here is the cause of such syndromes and not the actual physical manifestation of the disease. It is believed that daño is caused by means of a powerful potion which is either slipped into a drink or thrown across a doorstep late at night. A witch may be paid to cause a person magical harm by giving him or her ayahuasca. Some witches as well as ayahuasqueros are believed to control special spirits or familiars whom they can send to do evil or counteract evil magic. People believe that a *chonta* or thorn that carries disease-producing substances can be shot through the air by such witches at their enemies. As with all magical illness, it is imperative that a sick person suffering from daño seek a healer to neutralize the harm before it is fatal.

PULSARIO   An infirmity marked by symptoms of restlessness, hyperactivity, and free-floating anxiety, *pulsario* is sometimes described as a ball located at the mouth of the stomach which is painful and prevents normal digestive action. Informants say that this lump can be repressed pain, sorrow, or anger. Mainly attacking women, pulsario produces irritability and general unhappiness.

MAL DE OJO   Another disease syndrome found throughout Peru, *mal de ojo* is characterized by symptoms including nausea, vomiting, diarrhea, fever, loss of weight, insomnia, and sadness

(Valdivia 1964). In popular belief, the cause of the illness is the magical action of one person's glance upon the other, not necessarily with evil intentions in mind. Mal de ojo, however, can be motivated by envy. This illness is quite frequent among children, whose personal attractiveness may catch the evil eye. Mothers often place charms or amulets on the wrists or necks of their youngsters or exorcise them each day with tobacco smoke in the belief that they can ward off this disaster.

Ayahuasca Visions and Healing

The role of the ayahuasquero in healing such diseases is a central one. He must determine the origin of the illness before his patient can undergo any treatment. The healer must bring to light the cause of his patient's disease without the benefit of merely focusing upon a simple set of external symptoms. Once a sick person has found an ayahuasquero to treat him, both work together closely to analyze the visionary content of the drug experience to determine the agent responsible for the infirmity.

Informants often report vivid visions of forest creatures, especially boa constrictors and viperous snakes. Although some people claim that ayahuasca causes them no visual effects, most informants had visions filled with river and forest animals. Another frequent vision was that of the person believed responsible for bewitching the client. Others would report a panorama of activity in which some man or woman would express his innermost thoughts and feelings toward the patient, such as sexual desire, vengeance, or hate. At times, the vision is of an evil person manufacturing a potion and later throwing it across the victim's doorstep in the darkness.

As far as viperous snakes and boa constrictors are concerned, these fearsome creatures, which in any part of the world might be considered to be part of a "bad trip" phenomenon, are rather cleverly utilized by healers to help them in their curing. Interpreted as the reincarnated spirit of the vine itself, such mental productions are believed to bring messages of healing and assurance to the patient. If he or she is strong enough to withstand the fright and loss of ego control associated with such apparitions, the mother spirit of the vine will teach the patient her songs. During a successful session, one can observe patients who spontaneously break out into song, accompanying the healer or his apprentices (see Katz and Dobkin de Rios 1971). Although the physiological effects of hallucinogen use, ranging from states of euphoria to great anguish, without doubt have universal distribution (see Ludwig 1969), it is quite interesting to note how such potential "bad trips" can be minimized or controlled by healing techniques when the presence of a belief system sets such activity within an ongoing magical framework. Ayahuasca use is harnessed in such a way that the effects of culturally recognized frightening mental productions are controllable by the healer and actually used by him to effect a cure. This is not to say that bad trips do not occur with ayahuasca—I observed some cases when individuals shrieked in fright as viperous snakes and assorted demons appeared before them.

Mechanisms of Healing

The use of ayahuasca to heal does not include a conceptualization of the hallucinogen as a curative agent, per se. Rather, the vine is seen to operate as a powerful means to a desired end—it gives the healer entry into the culturally important area of disease causality, to enable him to identify the nature of the illness from which a person suffers, and then to deflect or neutralize the evil magic which was deemed responsible for illness. When we examine the successes attributed to the healer, we find that, in general, a selective process takes place so that curers accept patients only if they believe that they will have a good chance of success with them. Simple illnesses are rarely treated with the drug; herbs, plants, and store-bought medicines are prescribed by the healer for these types of affliction. Nor are psychotic patients given ayahuasca.

In addition to the use of the vine, a healer will practice time-honored Amazonian curing techniques including whistling, singing, recitation of orations, sucking at afflicted regions of the body, and blowing cigarette smoke over the patient's body. Ayahuasqueros, like other regional folk healers who do *not* use drugs, spend a good portion of their time in afternoon consultations using the above techniques, as well as visiting the homes of patients to advise, counsel, and reassure them.

The question arises in this kind of analysis: can we say that ayahuasca operates as a placebo? Is it possible that faith in the curative powers of the drug is enough to heal? It seems likely that we must dismiss this possibility. Ayahuasca is not used to gain verbal insight or to work through psychodynamic materials in order to effect long-range cures. Rather, the drug is used to identify the cause of magical illness. Ayahuasca visions change the generalized, immobilizing anxiety present in the sociocultural milieu into solid fear placed squarely on the shoulders of some evil-doer by a healer whose presentation of self includes an omnipotent stance. Certainly, if an aura of personal success surrounds such a healer, it can only add to the patient's belief that such a person is powerful enough to counter any evil magic. The drug, then, serves mainly diagnostic and revelatory purposes throughout.

Magical Conditioning

As one historian of medicine has pointed out, although irrational concepts of disease may be held in particular societies, nonetheless, many people do get cured (Gordon 1949). It is interesting to examine mechanisms of healing in Iquitos, where patients are drawn from civilized or transitional Indian groups and from middle-income segments of the community who seek help from ayahuasqueros only after other "rational" techniques have failed. Because of this mixed grouping in a given ayahuasca session, a capable healer, before allowing some of his patients to take the purge, will spend a period of up to two weeks exorcising the "evil" afflicting these individuals. This would seem to be a necessary part of the therapy, because of variant social realities. Magical beliefs among one segment function close to, and at times in competition with, rational ones. In order to alleviate the anxiety generated by the sensory overload inherent in drug ingestion, the healer, in a series of subtle ways, takes

an omnipotent stance vis-à-vis his patients. Should there be a
"doubting Thomas" present at the session, it is much less probable that the healer will be able to influence him while he is
under the effects of the drug. By means of the preparatory ex-
orcistic rituals (which may include the use of a local tobacco,
mapacho) healers present some of their patients with a learning
experience in order to permit them to come to terms with the
culturally determined expectations necessary for broad-based
success in a session. Patients' expectations that they will be visited by a boa or other snake, which they may have learned in
childhood or have had reinforced during these preliminary sessions, as well as their belief in the prediction of healing success
by that apparition, provide them with reassurance that healing
indeed is occurring. In many ways, the omnipotence of the
healer, which some writers see as crucial in explaining the efficacy of magical psychotherapies, is increased by the healer's
symbolic presentations—his insistence upon the magical world
of spirits that he controls, which he can conjure up through his
particular songs and whistling incantations. At ayahuasca sessions, one often hears a healer advising a patient who is experiencing difficult visions that the next song will cause something
to happen and that this bad moment will pass. Called upon as
a creative source to interpret the symbols that appear to his
patients, the healer sees in these productions elements that he
attributes to magical causality of misfortune or disease.

Doctrinal Compliance

Ehrenwald (1966), tracing the continuity between present-
day scientific therapy and so-called primitive healing, has coined
the phrase "doctrinal compliance." He analyzes the psychotherapeutic phenomenon that occurs frequently when a patient
does exactly what his doctor wants him to, regardless of the
particular school to which a psychiatrist may subscribe. If a
therapist, for example, is a Freudian, the patient's dreams often
tend to re-create early memories of childhood or family conflict.
At an unconscious level, then, the patient appears to be com-
plying with the therapist's unconscious wishes and expectations

in validating his theories. Unlike the phenomenon of suggestion, which operates on a conscious level, doctrinal compliance seems to be an unconscious process which occurs in both magical and modern therapy procedures. This would seem to be very pertinent to the ayahuasca healing situation, especially with regard to the exorcising of the patient, which marks a portion of modern healing in Iquitos.

Conclusion

The hallucinogen ayahuasca is used most effectively in healing those illnesses believed to be magical in origin. The particular visual hallucinations are put to use by the healer to determine the magical cause of illness as well as to neutralize evil magic. The importance of the forest setting and the widespread knowledge and familiarity of most people with the drug, their expectations of healing, and their respect for remembered cures of drug healers all point out the importance of cultural variables in understanding how hallucinogens have been used to augment healing.

Ayahuasca is used quite differently from the way Western drug-adjuncted psychotherapy was in the 1960s (see Caldwell 1968). In the latter, attempts were made within a Freudian dynamic framework to open up areas of repressed and painful memories. Long-term "psycholytic therapy" occurred where drugs were used over many months of treatment. Most ayahuasca healers see patients in a drug session for a relatively short period of time once the drug is administered, which can be repeated once or twice in a month or so, with little or no follow-up. Anxiety and stress, which are constant companions of many rain-forest slum dwellers, can reach intolerable levels, and the drug healer receives a call to ameliorate acute symptoms. It is in these ritual, magical healing sessions that ayahuasca is used most effectively—entering into the realm of tenuous, uneasy interpersonal relations and acting as a means to restore equilibrium in difficult situations.

Part 3

Cultural Universals and the Hallucinogens

Chapter 13

Cross-Cultural Motifs in the Use of Hallucinogenic Plants

If we reflect for a moment on the foregoing data, some important themes connected to the use of hallucinogens can be discerned easily, as can certain near-universal cultural similarities in drug-using societies. These similarities may be coincidental, or they may be due to direct borrowing of customs from one society to another. Or perhaps a third explanation is at work: it is possible that the biochemical properties of these drugs, which are still incompletely understood, may set the stage for similarities in cultural elaboration and symbolic representation. Thus, such physiological factors as increased pulse rate and the pounding of the heart (tachycardia) may find their way into the mytho-poetic cultural response of an aerial voyage or floating through the air that an individual may claim to experience as the result of drug ingestion. However, simple biochemical reductionism is not really the best solution. Durkheim long ago argued that social facts must have social explanations. That the human central nervous system is bombarded with biochemical input is not in question when we talk about the hallucinogens. What is interesting, however, is that each culture will elaborate the symbology connected to the drug experience in terms of the symbols and values of its own society, while at the same time having recourse to recurrent, universal sets of symbols. It is rare in the social sciences to find this kind of unified symbology, although some anthropologists have argued that natural symbols based on the human body constitute a major class for analysis.

Drug Use and the Sacred

One of the most striking motifs connected to drug use has to do with the division made in traditional societies between the realms of the sacred and the profane. Some writers have argued that in such societies a secular realm may not even be delineated. The feeling of terror, of awe-inspiring mystery, that individuals in such societies experience before the unknown certainly contrasts to the secular world view of people in a technologically advanced culture. The sacred in traditional society has often been manifested in the powers attributed to stones, trees, rivers, and the sky, which may have been revered because they permitted man a glimpse of the divine. Not only may such aspects of nature be consecrated in traditional societies, but powerful plants that bear messages of supernatural portent, too, easily fall within this realm.

Eliade (1957) has written that the major characteristic of the sacred is the way in which time is experienced. The experience of time among peoples of traditional society differs greatly from that of life in an industrialized world, where time is segmented to suit the society's needs. As Eliade describes sacred time, it is circular and reversible. In this philosophical view, an eternal mythical present exists which is periodically reintegrated into the religious rites of human beings. The properties of time suspension as it is experienced under the influence of plant hallucinogens can be seen to aid in reaffirming the sacred nature of man's sojourn on earth.

Animals and Hallucinogens

In several of the societies I have discussed, animals have played a vital role in teaching or revealing the properties of plant hallucinogens to human beings (see also Siegel 1973). From an evolutionary point of view, such activities are surprising. Although animals might occasionally eat fermented fruits that would make them drunk, or wander into tall grasses that they could eat without knowing that they were, for example, a species of Datura potent enough to cause disorientation, in general, animals would not be expected to seek out these plants. In a contrary mode, one could argue that this would be nonadaptive, since it would endanger the lives and reproductive success of any animal so involved. We can imagine the plight of an animal who ate a hallucinogenic mushroom or some other psychotropic plant and found himself immobilized and unable to recognize the normal cues that would signal nearby predators. On the positive side, however, such an animal might find his vision and, especially, his sense of smell heightened, which might indeed be of great use to him, provided that he could "pull himself together" and scamper out of danger if a predator happened along. Nonetheless, despite these obvious dangers, we note that among the Siberian shamans there is some indication that the reindeer's fondness for the fly agaric mushroom may have led human beings to experiment with the plant over time. In this way, people could tell at least that such an attractive-looking plant was not always poisonous. Perhaps the idea of drinking the urine of a mushroom user originated when people observed the interest of the reindeer in imbibing a man's urine after the animals fed on certain forest lichens. Reciprocal learning seems to have taken place in that the Siberian reindeer herdsmen used urine as a means of rounding up and corralling the animals upon which their livelihood depended. The drinking of urine did dilute the adverse somatic effects of the fly agaric mushroom, such as nausea, while permitting a more equitable sharing of the ecstasy encapsulated within the plant.

Another example of the relationship of human beings and animals with regard to drug ingestion can be found in the evidence available concerning the use of the mescal bean among the American Plains Indians. Informants reported that Indian groups found the red beans in the stomach of the deer that they hunted, which may give us some clues to the initial use of such plants by human beings. One can only imagine what must have happened to an unfortunate deer who ingested the powerful

red bean, whose potency is legendary. Perhaps the deer's in-
discretion led him into the snares of the ever-observant hunter.

Although the evidence is still not conclusive, it does permit
us to venture an educated guess about the role of animals in the
history of the human use of hallucinogens. We might indeed
expect that man, the hunter, paid particular attention to the
animals in his environment, that he observed their habits and
rhythms of life, and that he used this knowledge to increase his
hunting success. Contemporary ethnography details this bond
between man and animals, and points out very clearly how plant
hallucinogens were yet another means of cementing this relationship when such plants were available (see Dobkin de Rios
1972b).

A book by Cordova-Rios (Lamb and Cordova-Rios 1971) is
illustrative here. As a young Amazonian Mestizo, he claims to
have been captured by an Amahuaca rain forest group at the
end of the last century, and he became an ayahuasca-using shaman. The people among whom he lived used ayahuasca to help
them hunt. Taking advantage of the properties of this hallucinogenic vine, the adult men of the community re-created in their
visions the most minute, difficult movements and activities of
the animals they stalked and hunted. Their visions enabled them
to learn, once again in the conscious mind, the aspects of animal
behavior which they knew almost at a subliminal level, so that
in future hunts they could be at one with their prey to hasten
their victory. The mystical bond thus established between the
hunter and the animals he hunted would be strengthened by
whatever substance enabled him to increase and heighten his
perceptual capacities.* This is not to say that a hunter in the
tropical rain forest, for example, took ayahuasca and rushed out
to the hunt; such a hunter would be disoriented and would
probably just stumble in the underbrush. If, however, we rec-

---

*Carneiro (1980) has taken issue with Lamb's rendering of Cordova-
Rios's life as an ayahuasquero. In particular, the debate is over whether
Cordova-Rios was a liar and whether he spent time with Amahuaca
Indians from whom he claimed to have learned his craft of ayahuasca
healing.

ognize the use that was and still is made of hallucinogens in learning experiences, then we can see as adaptive the heightening of awareness of one's enemies and of potential prey, insofar as they increase man's ability to survive in hostile environments. I would argue that this aspect of drug use, as well as the possibility that human beings have learned about drug plants from animals, signifies great antiquity for such use of hallucinogens in the human record.

Some of my suggestions (1973) on the antiquity of plant hallucinogen ingestion have been verified independently by Ronald Siegel (personal communication), who examined the use of mind-altering plants by animals; by the late 1970s, he had documented more than 300 cases of animals ingesting plant hallucinogens. To Siegel, the data suggested that hallucinogenic plant ingestion could be set back in Paleolithic times, at least 40,000 years before present. During this period, human beings hunted and followed large beasts of prey. Depending upon their geographical location, these people were omnivorous in their eating habits. It is possible that hallucinogenic plants had great influence on the social life of such human beings.

Cultural Patterning of Visions

Another important theme, one of crucial importance to the historian of hallucinogen use, concerns the cultural patterning of visionary experience. Whether we consider the rain forest dweller taking ayahuasca to see his culture's heroes or creatures of his environment, or the Fang using iboga to see the Bwiti, we do learn how a most subjective experience, hallucination, can be culturally patterned and structured.

There seems to be good evidence that in a society where plant hallucinogens are used, each individual builds up a certain expectation of drug use which, in fact, permits the evocation of particular types of visions. That is not to say that if a group of adult men claim to see serpents appear before them, they all are actually viewing the same snake, as if they were attending a movie performance. Rather, what is at issue here is the cultural patterning of categories of visions—that is, how do one's expectations that a given kind of vision will occur make it, in fact, occur?

This aspect of hallucinogenic drug use is one that will continue to occupy anthropologists working in societies where such substances are used. People experience their membership in a culture at the deepest levels of awareness accessible through drug-induced experiences. Plant hallucinogens in traditional society can be said to have a thoroughgoing influence on the individual's unconscious. To summarize, we can argue that cultural identity is learned and reaffirmed by psychic productions under drug experiences in many traditional societies of the world. The evidence presented in this book indicates that substrata of the personality are highly susceptible to social learning. One would have to agree that any attempt to wrench the individual's psyche from its complex interrelationship with the cultural matrix is doomed to failure.

Aside from the psychological effects of drug use, we see from the data presented in this book that many of the societies exhibit belief systems that approach universality. For example, the belief in animated spirits of hallucinogenic plants recurs throughout the samples. In some societies, these spirit animators are miniscule; elsewhere, they may be gigantic. Psychiatric literature has described such visionary experiences with the terms micropsia and macropsia. One psychiatrist, Barber (1970), has argued that such universal reporting of small or very large figures in the wake of LSD-like experiences can be related to physiological phenomena that alter pupil activity in complex ways. In Lewis Carroll's *Alice in Wonderland* (1865), Alice ate one of two sides of a mushroom, either to grow larger or smaller. As the Wassons noted (1957), this probably was not coincidental. In the same year that Carroll's book appeared, a learned study of mushrooms carefully noted the properties of the fly agaric mushroom. Such hallucinogenic substances do seem to change the retinal image and permit the appearance of the geometric forms and patterns which are almost always reported in the wake of LSD-like-substance ingestion. In effect, these illusions may be the physiological structures in one's own visual system, including lattices, cones, cylinders, and other geometrics, suddenly amenable to observation under the effects of the drug.

Whether large or small, plant spirits or spirit helpers are believed to be dominated by drug-using shamans, who call upon these entities to cure or to bewitch. The shaman may call upon such forces to protect his community. At times, such spirit forces have been considered more powerful than man and have been viewed as a means of communicating with the realm of the supernatural, rather than experienced as forces which could be controlled.

If we look at the shamanistic use of hallucinogenic plants in this context, we see the frequently observed phenomenon of shamanic transformation into animal familiars (shape shifting, in folklore terminology), sent abroad to do the shaman's bidding, in order to rectify evil or to redress harm that has touched the life of the shaman's client. Amazonian shaman healers often boasted to me of their apprenticeship period when they obtained magical powers over their allies, a long, arduous, and, at times, lethal task. When the shaman is able to emerge triumphant from his training, he is believed to be possessed of impressive power. The shaman often descends to nether worlds to consult with ancestral spirits or else travels to celestial realms where he returns with special chants and auguries of future happenings. The metamorphosis of human beings into animals (or, less frequently, into plants) known as spirit familiars is a common, global drug-linked motif as well as a pan-American theme in general.

A particularly interesting symbolic transformation is that of the serpent, discussed at length by Mundkur (1976) in his studies of the cult of the serpent in the Americas. It is possible that the fear of poisonous snake venom is a symbolic association for the warrior capabilities of the shaman. This combative aspect of shamanism, portrayed particularly well among the Mochica, is another theme worth noting. Just as the serpent is able to defeat his enemies by the use of his venom, so, too, might the shaman, through his control over this animal familiar, be able to defeat an adversary. In my own studies of urban, drug-related shamanic healing in Peru, I found that such healers were as much

involved in strife with their perceived adversaries as they were
with contacting and controlling preternatural realms.

Mundkur points out that the importance of the serpent's
shedding its skin is a possible explanation for the high value
placed on this creature by different peoples throughout the world.
Often the drug-related theme of death and rebirth, or what Von
Winning (1969) has called the "life emerging from death" motif,
is found in PaleoIndian societies. The hallucinogenic experience
is often perceived as the death of the ego and the rebirth or
resurrection of the individual. In this manner, the shedding of
the serpent's skin may be matched with the death of the former
social role of the individual and the emergence of another. In
this context, it is not surprising to find the common use of
psychoactive plant drugs as part of puberty initiation rites (see
Johnston 1972).

Such powerful potentiators as plant hallucinogens lend
themselves to religious elaboration. Those individuals using them
often make the association of their "force" to cosmic powers.
The sample examined in this book includes beliefs in the capriciousness of such powers—the tricks that the powers play on
man and the impish things they do. However, in some respects,
this relationship between human beings and spirits of drug plants
may mirror the magician's psychic need for ontological security
to permit him to control the world in which he lives. The forces
or powers of a person's unconscious may, in other words, be
projected outward to the forces of nature to enable the drug-
using shaman to believe that his world is an understandable and
charted one and that he will not founder on its shoals. Insofar
as spirit helpers stereotypically seen in hallucinogenic visions
enable man to put on a good face and to go about the business
of hunting, staying alive, curing illness, and incapacitating his
enemies, then hallucinogenic drugs do seem to have been adaptive for human beings, at least from a psychological perspective.

Drug Use and Social Structure

As we have seen, revealed knowledge is highly valued in
traditional societies, especially those where hunting and gath-

ering are the main economic activities. Hierarchies of intermediaries who intercede between man and the supernatural may
be viewed as diluting and lessening the impact of the experience
of supernatural forces. By using plant hallucinogens, human
beings can strengthen the bond that exists between themselves
and their gods. Yet as societies grow in complexity and enter
into hierarchical orderings and segmentation, drug use and the
value placed on direct, mystical knowledge of the divine undergo
change.

We might expect that in simple, undifferentiated societies,
when drug plants are available their use would tend to be for
communal goods and ends. Global studies of plant hallucinogens indicate that with the advent of intensive agriculture and
the ensuing social structural complexity and segmentation, elite
segments of urban society usurp and manipulate hallucinogenic
plant use. They do so both for socially defined commonwealth
benefits and to control others. Access to specific states of consciousness is as much a part of sumptuary laws as access to fine
material goods, as Harner has pointed out (1970, personal communication). It may very well be that man's ability to bewitch
and to cause his enemy's death, which is believed to be part of
the power that comes from hallucinogenic plant use, can be
perceived as dangerous to members of stratified or state-level
society. We know that the concept of state society generally
means the total control over legitimized power, with all other
attempts at power being subject to regulation. If a peasant shaman in a state society were permitted to continue using drug
plants that were believed potent enough to bewitch a state ruler
or administrator, legitimate power might be viewed as in jeop-
ardy. It is possible that in the history of Western civilization,
ancient oracular use of hallucinogens disappeared because of
this threat to central authority. Certainly, the evidence of the
Aztec, Maya, and Inca is of interest here. As we have seen
(chapter 10, above), sumptuary laws attempting to limit the use
of coca to the Inca, his nobility, and favorites illustrate this principle. Among the Aztec and Maya, such a monopoly on drugs
by higher ranking segments of society may very well explain
the quick demise of drug knowledge upon contact with the West,

when a specialized caste of drug users was quickly eliminated. This esoteric knowledge did not again diffuse to the folk level where it surely originated.

The implications of loss of drug knowledge are interesting to examine. We might argue that reports of drug use in the past tended to dwell upon levels of society where hunting and gathering were prevalent, rather than upon larger populations in advanced civilizations, where only special castes may have employed the drug for communal or private ends. Indeed, as we have seen in the chapters on hunting and gathering societies, those groups with a shamanistic religious orientation make far more use of hallucinogens than do Old World agricultural societies (La Barre 1970b). Less technologically complex cultures use these drugs to obtain access to supernatural worlds. Nonetheless, it can be argued that the passage of time and the lack of documentary evidence may hide a history of ritual hallucinogenic use in Old World societies. Moreover, when drug knowledge is diffused among a large number of people in societies that are less complex or less stratified, such information tends to be passed on from generation to generation. When usurpation by an elite of special drug-related knowledge does occur, as appears to have happened in stratified societies like the Inca, this knowledge becomes much more volatile. It is quick to disappear in the face of subsequent culture change, such as conquest or colonial rule.

As a result, esoteric as opposed to exoteric rituals develop which are not generally diffused throughout the society. They are often coded cryptically in art forms which are difficult to decipher (see, for example, Dobkin de Rios 1974a). Reexamination of Old World art and artifacts in the light of data on ancient hallucinogenic use may reveal that psychoactive plants did influence religion in that hemisphere (Dobkin de Rios 1977a).

Recently, more data have become available on ancient Old World drug-using societies. At a 1973 conference on the cross-cultural uses of cannabis sponsored by the National Institute on Drug Abuse (see Rubin 1976), new ethnographic data were presented. Scholars such as Li (1975) are examining linguistic, archaeological, and historical documents to ascertain the role of plant hallucinogens such as cannabis and, to some extent, their influence on later philosophical systems of Old World civilizations such as China and Egypt (see Emboden 1979, 1981). One would expect that historical documents would not be much help in this endeavor, since the time line for Old World societies is so much greater than that of New World societies.

Another corollary theme that is worth recapitulating is how cultural value placed on revealed knowledge can be correlated with human beings' readiness to attribute supernatural powers to hallucinogenic plants. In those societies of the world where, for one reason or other, people have held that only firsthand experience is the true way to knowledge, such plants have been received with great acclaim and awe. As soon as hierarchical functionaries intercede between human beings, proposing doctrines concerning the supernatural and access to it, such plants either fall from popular use or else are taken away from folk segments. When these drugs are used as vehicles of direct access to the supernatural, they convey to each human being his own, personal vision of the supernatural while at the same time reaffirming the society's collective vision of truth and knowledge. In those societies where plant hallucinogens play a central role, one learns that the drug user believes that he or she can see, feel, touch, and experience the unknown—which is nevertheless filtered through a cultural screen of expected visionary experience.

Hallucinogens and Curing

Still another motif of interest is the way plant hallucinogens are used cross-culturally in the treatment of disease. This use is especially common among people who believe in a supernatural etiology of disease—a belief quite generalized among traditional populations. Thus, if one believes that most forms of disease and misfortune are due to the evil winning of others or to malignant forces of nature, the visionary content of hallucinogens can be used to identify the source of evil, which may be either a supernatural agent or an individual who has bewitched the sick person. Known and unknown faces can and do appear before the drug user; they can be blamed for whatever ill or misfortune is under scrutiny. Often, conflict and dislike of one's enemies bring to the mind's eye those very people whom it is easy to blame for one's misfortunes. Again, visionary content can be used for religious succor, for security against the unknown, and as a means of receiving auguries of the future.

Divination

Divinatory phenomena, too, are central to many of the ethnographic discussions. Why telepathy and precognition should accompany hallucinogenic drug use is still unanswerable. This aspect of drug use cannot be dismissed lightly. In modern American studies, anecdotal reports abound about the widespread appearance of paranormal phenomena among drug-using counterculture communes that were located throughout the United States in the 1970s. When ayahuasca was originally studied scientifically, two biochemists named its active principle *telepathine*, to honor its alleged divinatory powers. It is to be hoped that the years to come will shed more light on this topic by means of controlled studies. At any rate, the anthropological record affords us insights into such areas. Perhaps the idea gaining credence in Western intellectual circles thanks to the so-called new physics—namely that the Cartesian differentiation between subject and object may be logically assailable premises (see Zukav 1979)—will lead to careful studies in this area.

Preparation for Ritual Drug Use

Another theme that recurs through the empirical data is the importance of sexual abstinence and special preparatory diets prior to the ingestion of various plant hallucinogens. Sexual activity may be discouraged prior to the ritual ingestion of hallucinogenic plants because of a desire to channel libidinal energy toward interior states of contemplation. Any discharge of such energy might be viewed as detracting from the experience itself. The reason various drug-using societies are so particular about the food eaten before an individual ingests a hallucinogen may be due to a desire to heighten the effects of the drug when it is finally taken. An example may be the common taboo against salt ingestion. Although the biochemical effects of a lack of salt in the diet in tandem with the hallucinogenic experience are poorly understood, this is the kind of voluntary control of internal states that healers often attend to. At another level, however, the main effect of both sexual restraint and particular diets seems to be the shrouding of the actual experience in an aura of the unusual and the special. Thus when the initiate or the shaman comes to the experience, his expectation of entry into nonordinary realms of consciousness is heightened—and he is, in effect, psychologically as well as physically prepared for access to realms of the unconscious.

Ritualization

In connection with the foregoing, one of the most interesting aspects of non-Western hallucinatory plant use is the ritualization surrounding their use. Although pleasurable effects are not ignored, in the main such plants are ingested within the context of complex social ritual and ceremonialism. Societies such as those I have analyzed in this book use the plants to guide a person toward specific cultural goals. Among ancient hunters and gatherers, the horticulturalists or pastoral peoples of the world, the intensive farmers or members of early civilizations, and more recently, subcultures within industrial societies like the United States, the ritualization of behavior connected to drug ingestion is one of the near universals that we have available for study within an anthropological perspective.

THE FUNCTION OF RITUAL   While drug rituals are pervasive, their character and purpose vary. In an earlier publication (Dobkin de Rios and Smith 1977), I have examined the continuities and changes in their function and structure through examples both from traditional societies and from American society. My collaborator was Dr. David E. Smith, the founder of the Haight-Ashbury Free Clinic in San Francisco. The core of our hypothesis, based on Dr. Smith's analysis of the drug use patterns in American society and my own research on traditional drug use patterns cross-culturally, was that drug rituals develop in the absence of legal restrictions on their use. By intent or by coincidence, these rituals have served to control drug use.

We know that the web of legal restrictions which have been constructed to control drug use in Western societies, while useful in accomplishing that purpose, have also had undesirable consequences, some of them serious. Rituals, too, may have undesirable as well as desirable effects having to do with health hazards and the effects of the drugs consumed. The most common example is the ritualized passing of hypodermic needles, which frequently also passes along hepatitis.

While public policy in the United States today is directed toward criminalizing certain drug rituals in an effort to eliminate them, a lesson that we learn from the ritualization of drug use in traditional societies is that we should reexamine our approach to the control of certain psychoactive substances and consider the possible social benefit of certain specific rituals. Such scholars as Furst (1972), Meyerhoff (1975), and Zinberg, Jacobson, and Harding (1975) have shown how different types of drugs, such as marijuana, plant hallucinogens, and opiates, when controlled through drug rituals, have received support in emergent modern American subcultural groups as well as among traditional societies. Those authors, in fact, see a continuity in drug use rituals between modern American society and the traditional world, and argue that modern American drug rituals minimize undesirable drug effects.

Zinberg and Jacobson (1977) define ritual specifically connected to drug use as "stylized, prescribed behavior surrounding the use of a drug, the methods to procure and administer the drug, the selection of physical and social settings for use, activities after the drug is administered, and the methods of preventing untoward drug effects." They also look at social sanctions, which they define as norms that determine how or whether a particular drug should be used, including "informal and often unspoken values or rules of conduct by a given group" (1977: 4).

In contrast to these definitions, students of traditional societies have utilized others over the last several decades of anthropological theory building. A general overview of the function of ritual in human society, while not exhaustive in scope, can be applied to drug use and can allow us insight into the continuities and changes in man's use of psychoactive substances throughout human society. Students of cultural aspects of drug use have repeatedly noted the way in which such use in traditional societies is benign when there is ritual associated with its ingestion.

There are many purposes to human ritual behavior whether in industrial or preindustrial societies. Wallace (1966) defines ritual as an established or prescribed procedure for the performance of a religious or other formal or ceremonial act. While most drug use in traditional societies of the world occurs in a context of shared sacred meaning, the secularization of drug use in industrial societies does not mean that ritual plays an insignificant role there. In traditional societies, rituals tend to occur in religious contexts, in which human beings recognize a "more than human" realm with which they deal in a customary, prescribed fashion. But ritual can also be defined in secular terms to include any practice or pattern of behavior which is repeated in a prescribed manner. Some anthropologists have argued that belief and ritual go hand in hand, and usually cannot be separated. Belief serves to explain, rationalize, interpret, and direct the energy of the ritual performance. Lord Raglan (cited in Wallace 1966) argued that the purpose of ritual is to confer benefits upon or avert misfortunes from those by whom or on whose behalf the ritual is performed. It is effective because the actions and words produce a psychological effect upon the participants, although the words and actions in themselves may have no true esoteric value. A subject possibly worthy of exploration but not immediately germane to this discussion is the relationship between ritual pronouncements and hypnotic induction techniques (see Peters and Price-Williams 1980).

Kluckhohn viewed ritual as basically psychological in function. To him, ritual was an obsessive, repetitive action which symbolically dramatized the fundamental needs of a society— economic, biological, social, or sexual (1942: 78–79). Wallace specifies that all ritual is directed toward the problem of transforming human beings or nature. Its objective is to achieve a desired end or to prevent an undesired transformation from occurring. These ritual are labeled therapy/antitherapy rituals. Some rituals invoke supernatural beings, while others invoke an impersonal supernatural force or energy. Wallace views salvation as another purpose for ritual activity. Fear, rage, despair, and other intense emotions result when an individual's identity is threatened, or when his self-esteem is low. Given such a crisis situation, a salvation ritual can enable the victim to regain his sense of worth. As we saw in the chapter on ayahuasca use in the Amazon, mestizo men and women who used ayahuasca to obtain visions believed that they were viewing the individual who was responsible for causing them illness or misfortune. Ayahuasca healers utilize rituals to render ineffective the evil magic of ayahuasca-using witches who intended to harm their clients.

MUSIC AND DRUG-INDUCED ALTERED STATES OF CONSCIOUSNESS: THE JUNGLE GYM   The anxiety generated by rapid access to the unconscious may be expressed in such symptoms as nausea, diarrhea, cramps, tachycardia, and increased blood pressure. These components of the "bad trip" have been reported in all cultures for which adequate data are available. The pervasive presence of music as an integral part of the drug experience constitutes one of the most powerful rituals associated with the social management of altered states of consciousness. The evidence presented in table 5 shows the frequency with which music is used in New World drug rituals and attests to the crucial role of music when drugs provide access to extraordinary realms of consciousness.

The participant in the ritual perceives the structure of music quite differently from the way he would perceive it during normal waking consciousness. We know, of course, of the mathematical precision and structure that all music possesses, whatever the musical tonal system of a given culture or the repetition of musical phrases involved (see Lomax 1968; Hood 1971). What the ethnomusicologist Katz and I have argued (Katz and Dobkin de Rios 1971) is that once the biochemical effects of the hallucinogenic drug alter the user's perception, the music operates as a "jungle gym" for the consciousness during the drug state.

It provides a series of pathways and banisters through which the drug user negotiates his way. Here we are using metaphorically the familiar children's playground architectural structure, composed of iron bars interlinked in horizontal and vertical planes. In contrast, however, to the child's playtime structure, where the child can choose spontaneous pathways and heights to explore, we suggest that the companionship of music to the hallucinogenic drug experience functions almost like a computer's magnetic tape. It can instruct the calculating machine in a particular course to follow. The cultural patterning of hallucinogen-induced visions suggests that the mathematical structure of music may serve specific cultural goals—to allow the drug taker to see the guardian spirit of the ayahuasca vine, to achieve contact with a special supernatural deity, and so forth. To reiterate, the jungle gym is an inflexible system where the choice of pathway is left to the child, whereas music, also a fixed structure, is imposed upon the drug user by the shaman, who controls to some degree his client's visual options within this ritualized use of music.

If we look at table 5, we see variations in drug-adjuncted music. This generally unstudied area in anthropology is one that merits particular attention. One general characteristic of the musics, or their lowest common denominator, appears to be the frequency of rattling effects or rapid vibratory sounds, almost always in consort with whistling or singing. Rattles, singing, chanting, and vocal productions, in general, may be a very important part of the hallucinogenic experience in that the "jungle gym" is built up, torn down, and rearranged, in a sort of "block-building" of consciousness to serve specific cultural goals.

As Ludwig pointed out (1969), synesthesias are commonly reported by drug users. I would like to stress that in most traditional drug-using societies, this scrambling of sensory modalities is not only recognized, but actually underpins the programming of rituals so as to heighten all sensory modalities. The data summarized in table 5 suggest that visual, olfactory, tactile, auditory, and gustatory senses are affected by the music. Even in relatively undramatic drug sessions similar to the many that I observed in Peru, sensory overload is preponderant in the drug experience and can provide a subjective drama, as distinct from an external thespian flavor. In other parts of the world, however, and even among Amazonian hunters and gatherers, the use of dancing, vivid body paint, bird feathers of bright hue, and so on, add to the sensory overload.

DRUG USE AND LIMINALITY   Although a major function of ritual is to allay the anxiety that can result from ingesting hallucinogens, not all drug rituals have as their function to rectify distress. Kluckhohn (1942) has argued that rituals are adaptive in human society insofar as they promote social solidarity, bringing people together into situations in which quarreling is ordinarily considered bad form. Another explanation for ritual has been offered by Rappaport (1971), who sees it as an information-exchange device that communicates cultural, ecological, and demographic data across the boundaries of local social groups. Such information can be used in planning short-range ecological and social strategies. The relationships among different groups within a bounded environment may be more adaptive when the individuals interact occasionally according to formal rules. The case of the Australian Aborigines is a good example here, where the use of pituri in a ritualized fashion may have minimized disruptive antisocial tendencies. Anthropologists such as Aberle, in discussing peyote use among the Navajo (1966), and Fernandez (1972), in discussing the Bwiti cult activities, will accept the positive role that drug use had among those populations faced with cultural disorganization.

Another set of rituals are those of "liminality," or marginality, in rites of passage. People who are in the process of changing their social state leave behind them the artifacts, identity, and names of past times. People in both traditional and modern societies publicly proclaim their movement from one social status to another by means of standardized rituals. In traditional societies, plant hallucinogens are often part of the rituals involved in these liminal stages, during which time those making a transition are segregated from the larger society, and the process of transformation occurs formally. Johnston (1972) shows how *Datura fatuosa* use among a girls' puberty school in Tshogana Tsonga society in Mozambique is an integral part of the ritual, allowing

Table 5. *Music and Hallucinogen-Induced Altered States of Consciousness.*

Society	Type of Music	Ritual and/or Function	Drug Used	Comments	Who Performs	Bibliography
Tukano Indians, Colombia	panpipes, gourd rattles, large wooden tube drum, singing, dancing	recitation of myths, conversation, singing, to commemorate creation myth; reaffirmation of strict exogamy laws; shamanistic initiation; maintain traditions; teach religious knowledge; maintain psychological equilibrium	Piptadenia; Vilho snuff, tobacco; Banisteriopsis spp.; Yajé (Spanish)	myths recited in hypnotic tone with great precision and insistence; women observe and sing; ritual conversations, greeting sunrise; total body painted red; singing and dancing; feather adornment; some ritualized gestures; jumping while walking	shaman (payé); adult males and boys; shaman and novice	Reichel-Dolmatoff 1971: 16, 128–29, 131, 133, 251; 1972: 88–90, 97, 101
Yanomamö, Venezuela and Brazil	chants, rattle, singing	to induce ritual death, envision familiars; invitation to hekura spirits to come and dwell in man's chest; to make contact with and attempt to control hekura shamanistic initiation; curing and control of spirits causing illness	tobacco; Virola; ebené (vernacular)	some individual body decoration with feathers for ritual feasts; prancing, back and forth in front of the house; dancing, shouting with weapons over head; chest pounding and ear shouting duels sometimes follow; strong odors used to stop bad experiences	adult males; shamans	Chagnon 1968: 23–24, 90–91, 109, 150–51; Prance 1970: 64–68
Aztec, Mexico	dancing, singing, and weeping	take initiatory journey to end of world; celebration of joy; political occasions to solidify alliances in divinatory feast	Psilocybe, strophalia and conocybe spp.; teonanactl (nahuatl)	all day and night festival with song and dance; visions of dying, being eaten by wild beasts, capturing prisoners in war, being rich, having wives or committing adultery and being executed; visions shared and discussed	nobility; visiting dignitaries	Guerra 1971: 116; ibid, cited in Schultes 1972: 14–15
Luiseño, California	dancing, wild screaming	initiation rites; adolescents put into frenzy and stupor to find out about adult life	Datura spp.	none	young men and adolescents	Schultes 1972a: 47
Tenetehara Indians, Brazil	dancing, chanting, shaking rattle, native ritual music, whistling bell, fervent music, and song	curing ritual, to call spirit to aid in curing; call upon Virgin Mary to intercede in illness	tobacco; Cannabis	intoxication from smoke, rhythm of song and dance	shaman	Wilbert 1972: 56
Mestizos, North Coast Peru	whistling, songs, occasional use of conch shell	shamanistic all night curing ceremony	Trichocereus pachanoi; San Pedro (Spanish); Datura arborea; condorillo spp. hornamo, tobacco	prayers and invocations and chants accompanied by rhythmic beat and traditional shamanistic rattle; symbolic contact and all of patients' senses stimulated; to relieve magically caused disease; to bewitch enemy; perfume drunk by patient	folk healer; patients	Sharon 1972a: 43–44; 1972b: 128–29; Dobkin de Rios 1968a: 193–94; 1968b: 42–43; 1973: 69–70, 80
Navajo Indians, United States	drums, singing, whistling, rattles	curing ceremony, averting evil and promoting future good; to thank God for past blessing; communication with supernatural	Lophophora williamsii, peyote	all-night ritual; prayer, song, drumming, eating peyote; cedar incense; ritual cigarettes smoked; communal drinking of water and corn meal at dawn; light from small fire only	communicants, both men and women	Aberle 1966: 11, 125–53

211

Table 5, continued.

Society	Type of Music	Ritual and/or Function	Drug Used	Comments	Who Performs	Bibliography
Chama Indians, Upper Amazon	songs, hissing sounds, guttural noises	curing sessions; shamanistic initiation to acquire supernatural power	ayahuasca; *Banisteriopsis*; tobacco juice	secluded locale at night; visions changed with chants of song; spirit of tobacco appears to novice shaman and teaches him his song	curer, initiate	Kusel 1965: 62–65; Elick 1969 cited in Wilbert 1972: 14–17
Cashinahua Indians, SE Peruvian Amazon	chanting, singing	communal ceremony, to learn about things removed in time and space; divinatory; to cure disease	*Banisteriopsis* spp. Nixi pae; ayahuasca	evening ritual; rhythmic swaying of bodies while sitting in group; singing individually; songs not coordinated	initiated males; shaman and other participants	Kensinger 1972: 9–13, 14
Menomini, Wisconsin	songs, drumming	to obtain power from the great spirit, relief from problems of illness	*Lophophora williamsii*, peyote	ceremony varies from serious intense to quite emotional; songs cry for help and prayers; pleas for salvation and for aid and relief from doubts, fears, guilt feelings	cult members	Spindler 1955: 433–44
Huichol, Mexico	guitar, fiddling, singing, trumpet, horns	peyote quest, ritual obtaining of peyote, reciting ancient stories	*Lophophora williamsii*, peyote	initiated sing and dance while novices ingest peyote	men, women, and children	Furst 1972: 177–78, 180–81
Mazatec Indians, Mexico	singing, drumming on body, forehead and arms; clapping hands	curing ceremony, to diagnose illness	*psilocybe, stropharia* and *conocybe* spp. mushrooms	darkened area except for fire embers; incense burning in small hut; curer's song experienced from all over hut	curer (men and women), ceremonial participants	Wasson 1972: 197–98; Munn 1973: 88, 90, 91, 111
Jivaro Indians, E Ecuador	drumming on hollowed log, singing and whistling	soul stealing; curing; to capture soul of enemy so as to leave him vulnerable to attack and death; trance state achieved to contact supernatural world; remove bewitching object from patient's body	*Banisteriopsis* spp. natema; tobacco juice; *Datura arborea*; *Datura sauveolens*	drinking quantities of natema; beating drum and repeating name of intended victim; ritual singing; sucking and social interaction in darkness	shaman and patient	Harner 1973a: 141, 153–54, 160–61; Harner 1973b: 15, 23
Sharanahua, Peruvian Amazon	songs, chants	curing ceremony, seeking vision to show cause of illness	*Banisteriopsis* spp., ayahuasca	evening sessions; establishing social solidarity	shaman; adult men	Siskind 1973: 28, 31–38
Culina, Peruvian Amazon	singing	curing magically caused illness	*Banisteriopsis* spp., ayahuasca	none	curer	Riviere and Lindgren 1972: 102
Amahuaca Indians, Upper Amazon	chants	curing sessions; prophesy to maintain social solidarity; to locate animals, enemies	*Banisteriopsis* spp., honi kuma	trancelike atmosphere produced by chanting; faces painted	adult men	Lamb and Cordova-Rios 1971: 26, 37–39, 148, 157, 165, 167–68
Kiowa Indians, Comanche Indians, United States	chants	ceremony to pray, meditate at all-night meetings	*Lophophora williamsii*, peyote	no dancing; ending with communal meal	unknown	Schultes 1972a: 14–15

the initiates to achieve union with the fertility god, and to sacralize their change of social status, and to formulate potentially unlimited series of alternative social arrangements. Turner (1974) applies the term *communitas* to the bonds in society that are antistructural, undifferentiated, egalitarian, direct, and nonrational, as opposed to the more formal "establishment" structures that hold people apart. In Turner's view, the drama of ritual action, including the use of plant hallucinogens, is an important characteristic of communitas. Liminality within rites of passage is opposed to the concept of social structure and gives rise to a state of "outsiderhood," a group set outside the structural arrangements of a given social system.

OTHER ASPECTS OF RITUAL   Some drug rituals, of course, are unpleasant. In some traditional societies we have seen that the use of mind-altering plants within an ethos of combat and violence is quite common, and such plants can be and have been used for bellicose and aggressive purposes. In Aztec society, discussed earlier, where at least four major plant hallucinogens were recorded, such substances served political functions in cementing alliances between the Aztec and subordinate rival states, but were also used by war captives prior to being sacrificed. By the same token, both Nazca and Mochica drug ingestion were probably integrated ritually into the power needs of individual political-religious regional leaders.

Ritual use of psychoactive drugs in traditional societies has sometimes been accompanied by overdosing. Fernandez, who worked with Bwiti cult members, showed that puberty rituals sometimes included deaths resulting from enthusiastic dosing of drug takers. The social benefits of rituals could be said to outweigh the occasional individual casuality, since mind-altering drugs were used as a means to ensure conformity with a society's religious goals and to achieve union with divinity. These aims may have been more important to the social group in reinforcing its solidarity than an occasional death.

An important aspect of the ritualization of drug use is the question of what happens to a society into which new psychoactive drugs have been introduced. The Australian Aborigines are a good example. They utilized one psychoactive drug,

pituri, in a controlled, ritualized fashion, but when Westerni-
zation and missionization made pituri less available to them,
they turned to alcohol use and experienced a high incidence of
adverse reactions, presumably because it was introduced without any rituals to control its role in society.

We cannot understand the use of drugs in human society
without considering the function of the rituals that have been
integral to such use. Some rituals have tended to control use
and reduce complications; others may have been inimical to the
well-being of the user. We need to look at the adaptive value of
a behavior, that is, how it may have contributed to the group's
ability to survive, in order to evaluate it usefully. Certainly, Har-
ris has paved the way in this type of analysis for more than a
decade (see especially 1974).

The anthropological contribution to the study of sacred plants
is summarized in figure 30, which shows that the social scientist
can view the interaction of variables and effects of the hallucinogen in order to predict the drug effect.

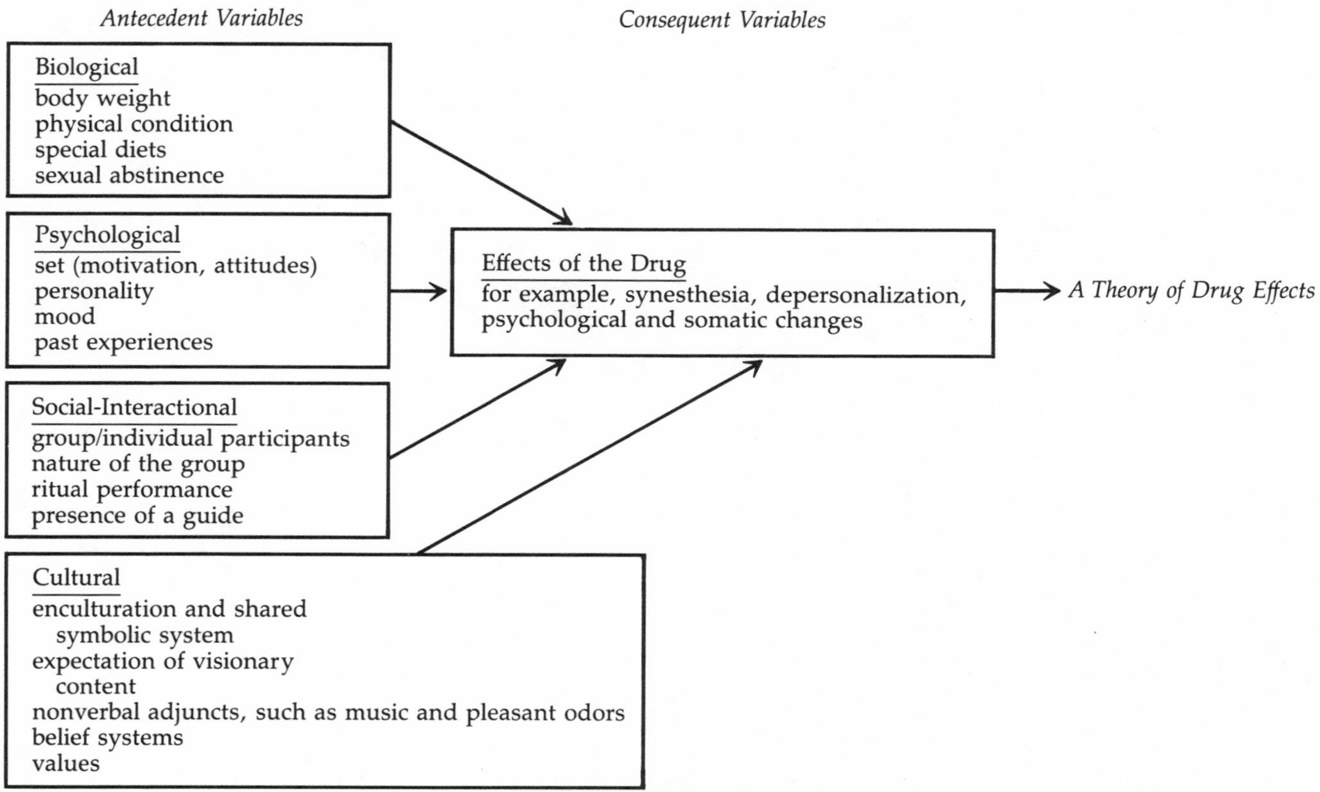

Figure 30. Schema of drug-induced visionary experience.

Chapter 14

Summary and Conclusions

As these studies of the cultural use of mind-altering plants in traditional society have shown, it is clear that plant hallucinogens, in one form or another, have been part of the human experience from the beginning. If anything, the data in this book would tend to substantiate a greater antiquity for the use of such plants than generally conceded. Yet, despite the proposed antiquity of such plants we find little, if any, abuse. In this case, abuse is defined as the sense of danger either to health or society. As Blum has pointed out in a study of over 247 societies in the Human Relations Area Files (1969), abuse is nil when self-reports of informants are considered. When Westerners have commented on drug use in a society, even within the confines of their own cognitive systems, they have generally acknowledged that the substances did not threaten native cultures. The disdainful accounts of various Spanish prelates in the wake of the Conquest focus upon the difficulties of converting native Americans to Christianity (Guerra 1971).

The misuse of drugs in traditional society has generally taken the form of witchcraft aimed at harming someone's enemies for a fee. So-called hedonistic aspects of drug use generally entailed the enhancement of interaction among strangers or members of a social group. For example, in a sample of 144

217

societies of hunters and gatherers, Blum found that hallucinogens were used for escape in less than 1 percent of the cases.
Generally, social or interpersonal, other-oriented settings are the
ones in which plant hallucinogens are used. In all cases, where
members of a society merely indulge in a plant recreationally,
we tend to find European influence, cultural disorganization,
and concomitant problems of alienation and alcoholism.

Moreover, when plant hallucinogens are used in traditional
society, they often take on the aspect of a learning experience.
Thus among rain-forest hunters and gatherers such as those
described by Lamb and Cordova-Rios (1971), we saw how learning the ways of animals to permit greater success in the hunt
was a major function of ayahuasca use. No doubt other marginal
peoples in the past have used such plants because of their ability
to heighten sensory perception and to permit a person to recall
memories only partially available to ordinary consciousness.

In those societies for which adequate data exist, we have
noted the cultural patterning of hallucinatory experience, which
gives us a fascinating glimpse into the extent to which the human
psyche is subject to cultural conditioning. This is interesting to
the student of drug abuse in industrial society, who finds that
the opposite generally obtains: namely, visionary content is particularly idiosyncratic and nonpatterned. In traditional societies,
stereotypic visions are eagerly sought after, to indicate that contact with the realm of the sacred is occurring. Certainly, as the
data show, the use of plant hallucinogens for the reduction of
private anxiety, the easing of personal problems, or a general
avoidance of responsibility and escape from social pressures seems
to occur only in the case of the Kuma. Nonetheless, in that New
Guinean society, we saw an institutionalized expression of structural stress. When the mushrooms were ingested, a cultural
drama unfolded and individual stress was released in a particular manner. For the most part, in the societies we have considered, drugs are used in a magical-religious sense, within a
ceremonial context, to celebrate or to contact the realm of the
supernatural, to heal an illness, to diagnose its cause, to divine
the future, or to promote social solidarity among men and women.

Throughout human history, the power of mind-altering plants

has been acknowledged to belong to special realms constrained with taboos and rituals. Any man who dared to enter those portals had to be properly prepared for the journey. The sacred nature of plant hallucinogens in non-Western society can only attest to the maturity and the experience of individuals in such societies who dealt with hallucinogenic plants in their rituals, integrating realms of inner experience and feelings with their natural and interpersonal milieu.

References

ABERLE, D. F.
1966   *The Peyote Religion Among the Navaho,* Viking Fund Publications
        in Anthropology, no. 42 (Chicago: Aldine Publishing Co.).
ACKERKNECHT, E.
1971   *Medicine and Ethnology. Selected Essays* (New York: International
        Publications).
ALTSCHUL, S. V. R.
1964   "A Taxonomic Study of the Genus Anadenanthera," *Contribu-
        tions of Gray Herbarium* 193: 3–65 (Harvard University).
1971   *The Genus Anadenanthera in Amerindian Cultures,* Harvard Uni-
        versity Botanical Museum Leaflets (Cambridge, Mass.).
ANONYMOUS
1978   "Nuevas Perspectivas en Torno al Debate Sobre el Uso de la
        Coca," *América Indígena* 38: 4.
ARISTOTLE
1961   *Poetics,* trans. S. H. Butcher (New York: Hill and Wang).
ATKINSON, R.
n.d.   "Out-of-the-Body Experiences: A Critical Review of the Phe-
        nomenon and Discussion of Theoretically Possible Mechanisms
        for Its Occurrence," unpublished manuscript (University of Cal-
        ifornia, Irvine).
BALANDIER, G.
1957   *Ambiguous Africa: Cultures in Collision* (Paris: Plon).

1963   *Sociologie Actuelle de l'Afrique Noire* (Paris: Presses Universitaires de France).

BANFIELD, EDWARD

1958   *The Moral Basis of a Backward Society* (Glencoe, Ill.: Free Press).

BARBER, T. X.

1970   *LSD, Marihuana, Yoga and Hypnosis* (Chicago: Aldine Publishing Co.).

BARRET, P.

1932   "Le Yagé," *Société des Americanistes de Paris* 24: 309–10.

BARRON, F., ET AL.

1964   "The Hallucinogenic Drugs," *Scientific American* 210(4): 29–37.

BASEDOW, H.

1925   *The Australian Aborigines* (Adelaide, Australia: Preece & Sons).

BENEDICT, RUTH

1922   "The Vision in Plains Culture," *American Anthropologist* 24: 1–23.

BENNETT, W. C., AND J. B. BIRD

1946   "The Archaeology of the Central Andes," in *Handbook of South American Indians,"* ed. J. Steward, vol. 2, *The Andean Civilizations* (Washington, D.C.: Smithsonian Institution).

BENNETT, WENDEL C., AND ROBERT ZINGG

1935   *The Tarahumara: An Indian Tribe of Northern Mexico* (Chicago: University of Chicago Press).

BENSON, ELIZABETH

1972   *The Mochica* (New York: Praeger).

1974   *A Man and a Feline in Mochica Art*, Dumbarton Oaks Studies in Pre-Columbian Art and Archaeology 14 (Washington, D.C.).

BERNDT, CATHERINE

1964   "The Role of Native Doctors in Aboriginal Australia," in *Magic, Faith, and Heaing*, ed. A. Kiev (New York: Free Press).

BETTELHEIM, BRUNO

1954   *Symbolic Wounds* (Glencoe: Free Press).

BLASCO, M., AND L. J. RAMOS

1974   "Cabezas Cortadas en la Cerámica Nazca según la Colección del Museo de América de Madrid," *Cuadernos Prehistóricos* 2(2), Seminario Americanista de la Universidad de Valladolid.

BLUM, RICHARD

1964   *Drugs and Society*, vol. 1 (Stanford, Calif.: Jossey-Bass).

BOGORAS, W.

1910   "The Chukchee," in *Memoirs of the American Museum of Natural History* 12: 205–7.

BOLTON, R.
1979   "On Coca Chewing and High Altitude Stress," *Current Anthropology* 20: 418–20.

BOURGUIGNON, E.
1973   *Religion, Altered States of Consciousness, and Social Change* (Columbus: Ohio State University Press).

BOWER, GORDON H.
1981   *Theories of Learning*, 5th ed. (Englewood Cliffs, N.J.: Prentice Hall).

BRADEN, CHARLES
1930   *Religious Aspects of the Conquest of Mexico* (Durham, N.C.: Duke University Press).

BRAY, WARWICK, AND COLIN DOLLERY
1983   "Coca Chewing and High Altitude Stress: A Spurious Correlation," *Current Anthropology* 24(3): 269–82.

BROOKS, J. E., ED.
1938   *Tobacco, Its History Illustrated by the Books, Manuscripts and Engravings in the Library of George Arents, Jr.*, vol. I, 1507–1615 (New York: Rosenbach).

BROWN, KENNETH L.
1984   "Hallucinogenic Mushrooms, Jade, Obsidian, and the Guatemalan Highlands: What Did the Olmecs Really Want," in *Trade and Exchange in Early Mesoamerica*, ed. K. G. Hirth (Albuquerque: University of New Mexico Press).

BUSHNELL, G. S.
1965   *Ancient Arts of the Americas* (New York: Praeger).

CALDERON, E., AND DOUGLAS SHARON
1978   *Terápia de la Curandería* (Trujillo, Peru: Edigraf).

CALDWELL, W. V.
1968   *LSD Psychotherapy: An Exploration of Psychedelic and Psycholytic Therapy* (New York: Grove Press).

CAMPBELL, T. N.
1958   "Origin of the Mescal Bean Cult," *American Anthropologist* 60: 156–60.

CARNEIRO, ROBERT L.
1980   "Chimera of the Upper Amazon," in *The Don Juan Papers: Further Castaneda Controversies*, ed. R. de Mille (Santa Barbara, Calif.: Ross-Erikson).

CARROLL, LEWIS
1865   *Alice's Adventures in Wonderland* (London: Macmillan & Co.).

CASO, ALFONSO
1958   *The Aztecs: People of the Sun,* trans. Lowell Dunham (Norman: University of Oklahoma Press).
CAWTE, J. E.
1964   "Australian Ethnopsychiatry in the Field. A Sampling in N. Kimberley," *Medical Journal of Australia* 1: 467–72.
CHAGNON, NAPOLEON
1968   *Yanomamo: The Fierce People* (New York: Holt, Rinehart & Winston).
CLELLAND, J. B.
1966   "Ecology, Environment and Diseases," in *Aboriginal Man in South and Central Australia* (Adelaide: Government Printing Office).
COBO, B.
1956   *Obras de Padre B. Cobo,* vol. 1 (Madrid).
COE, MICHAEL
1966   *The Maya* (New York: Praeger).
1971   "The Shadow of the Olmecs," *Horizon* 13(4): 67–74.
COOK, S. F.
1946   "Sacrifice and Warfare as Factors in the Demography of Pre-Colonial Mexico," *Human Biology* 18: 81–102.
COOPER, J. M.
1949   A Cross-cultural Survey of South American Indian Tribes: Stimulants and Narcotics," in *Handbook of South American Indians,* ed. J. Steward, vol. 5 (Washington, D.C.: Smithsonian Institution).
CUZIN, J.
1967   Chemical Abstracts 66: 92491.
DALY, J. W., AND B. WITKOP
1971   "Chemistry and Pharmacology of Frog Venoms," *Venomous Animals and Their Venoms* 2: 497–519.
DAVIS, E., ET AL.
1969   "Effects of Harmine on the Cat's Visual System," *Anatomical Record* 163(2): 175.
1970   "Alteration of Flash-Induced Responses by Intra-carotoid Administration of Harmine," *Federation Proceedings of the American Society for Experimental Biology* (Abstracts), p. 454.
DE BORHEGYI, S.
1961   "Miniature Mushroom Stones from Guatemala," *American Antiquity* 26: 328–38.
1963   "Pre-Columbian Pottery Mushrooms from Mesoamerica," *American Antiquity* 28: 328–38.

1965   "Archaeological Synthesis of the Guatemalan Highlands," in *The Handbook of Middle American Indians*, ed. R. Wauchope, vol. 2 (Austin: University of Texas Press).

DELAY, J.

1967   "Psychopharmacology and Psychiatry: Towards a Classification of Psychotropic Drugs," *Bulletin on Narcotics* 19(1): 1–6.

DELLA SANTA, E.

1962   *Les Vases Peruviens de la Collection de LL. MM. le Roi Albert et la Reine Elisabeth de Belgique* (Brussels: Musees Royaux d'Art et d'Histoire, Dept. de l'Ethnographie).

DEL POZO, E.

1967   "Empiricism and Magic in Aztec Pharmacology," in *Ethnopharmacologic Search for Psychoactive Drugs*, ed. D. Efron (Washington, D.C.: U.S. Government Printing Office).

DE VECIANA, A.

1958   *La Secta del Bwiti en la Guinea Española* (Madrid: Instituto de Estudios Africanos, Consejo Superior de Investigaciones Científicas).

DIAZ, JOSE L.

1976   "Etnofarmacología de Algunos Psicotrópicos Vegetales de México," in *Etnofarmacología de Plantas Alucinógenas Latinoamericanas*, ed. J. L. Diaz (Mexico City: Centro Mexicano de Estudios en Farmacodependéncia–CEMEF).

DISSELHOFF, H. D.

1967   *Daily Life in Ancient Peru*, trans. A. Jaffe (New York: McGraw-Hill).

DOBKIN DE RIOS, MARLENE

1968a   "Folk Curing with a Psychedelic Cactus in Northern Peru," *International Journal of Social Psychiatry* 15: 23–32.

1968b   *"Trichocereus pachanoi*—A Mescaline Cactus Used in Folk Healing in Peru," *Economic Botany* 22(2): 194–99.

1970   *"Banisteriopsis* Used in Witchcraft and Folk Healing in Iquitos, Peru," *Economic Botany* 24(35): 296–300.

1971   "Ayahuasca, the Healing Vine," *International Journal of Social Psychiatry* 17(4): 256–69.

1972a   "Curing with Ayahuasca in a Peruvian Amazon Slum," in *Hallucinogens and Shamanism*, ed. M. J. Harner (New York: Oxford University Press).

1972b   *Visionary Vine: Psychedelic Healing in the Peruvian Amazon* (San Francisco: Chandler Publishing Co.).

1973 "Peruvian Hallucinogenic Folk Healing: An Overview," in *Psychiatry: Proceedings of the Fifth World Congress of Psychiatry*, vol. 2, ed. R. de la Fuente and M. Weisman (Mexico City).

1974a "The Influence of Psychoactive Flora and Fauna on Maya Religion," *Current Anthropology* 15(2): 147–64.

1974b "Cultural Persona in Drug-Induced Altered States of Consciousness," in *Social and Cultural Identity: Problems of Persistence and Change*, ed. T. Fitzgerald, Proceedings of the Southern Anthropological Society, no. 8 (Athens: University of Georgia Press).

1975 "Man, Culture and Hallucinogens: An Overview," in *Cannabis and Culture* (The Hague: Mouton Press).

1976 "Suggested Hallucinogenic Motifs in New World Massive Earthworks," in *Drugs, Rituals and Altered States of Consciousness*, ed. B. du Toit (Amsterdam: Balkema Press).

1977a "Comment on the Cult of the Serpent in the Americas," *Current Anthropology* 18(3): 556–57.

1977b "Plant Hallucinogens and the Religion of the Mochica—An Ancient Peruvian People," *Economic Botany* 31(2): 189–203.

1978 "The Maya and the Water Lily," *The New Scholar* 5(2): 299–309.

1979 "Hallucinogenic Ritual as Theatre," *Journal of Psychoactive Drugs* 9(3): 265–68.

1982 "Plant Hallucinogens, Sexuality and Shamanism in the Ceramic Art of Ancient Peru," *Journal of Psychoactive Drugs* 14(1–2): 81–90.

DOBKIN DE RIOS, MARLENE, AND MERCEDES CARDENAS

1980 "Plant Hallucinogens, Shamanism and Nazca Ceramics," *Journal of Ethnopharmacology* 2(3): 233–46.

DOBKIN DE RIOS, MARLENE, AND FRED KATZ

1975 "Some Relationships Between Music and Hallucinogenic Ritual: The Jungle Gym in Consciousness," *Ethos* 3(1): 64–76.

DOBKIN DE RIOS, MARLENE, AND DAVID E. SMITH

1977 "Drug Use and Abuse in Cross-cultural Perspective," *Human Organization* 36(1): 15–21.

DONNAN, CHRISTOPHER B.

1976 *Moche Art and Iconography*, UCLA Latin American Series, vol. 33 (Los Angeles).

DRIVER, HAROLD

1961 *Indians of North America* (Chicago: University of Chicago Press).

DURAN, D.

1964 *The Aztecs: The History of the Indies of New Spain*, trans. D. Heyden and F. Horcastias (New York: Orion).

EASTWELL, H. D.

1982a "Australian Aboriginal Mental Health: An Overview," in *Transcultural Psychiatric Research Review* 19:221–47.

1982b "Voodoo Death and the Mechanism for Dispatch of the Dying in E. Arnhem," *American Anthropologist* 84(1): 5–18.

EFRON, DAVID, ED.

1967 *Ethnopharmacologic Search for Psychoactive Drugs*, Public Health Service Publication no. 1645 (Washington, D.C.: National Institute of Mental Health).

EHRENWALD, JAN

1966 *Psychotherapy: Myth or Method?* (New York: Grune and Stratton).

EISNER, BETTY

1967 "The Importance of the Non-verbal," in *The Use of LSD in Psychotherapy and Alcoholism*, ed. H. Abramson (New York: Bobbs-Merrill).

ELIADE, MIRCEA

1957 *The Sacred and the Profane*, trans. W. Trask (New York: Harcourt Brace).

1958 *Shamanism: Archaic Techniques of Ecstasy*, trans. W. Trask (New York: Pantheon Books).

1975 *Myths, Rites and Symbols* (New York: Harper and Row, Publishers).

EL-ZOGHBY, S. M., ET AL.

1970 "Studies on the Effect of Reserpine Therapy on the Functional Capacity of the Tryptophan-Niacin Pathway in Smoker and Non-Smoker Males," *Biochemical Pharmacology* 19: 1661–67.

EMBODEN, WILLIAM A.

1979a *Narcotic Plants* (New York: Macmillan Publishing Co.).

1979b "The Sacred Narcotic Lily of the Nile: *Nymphaea Caerulea Sav.*," *Economic Botany* 33: 274–81.

1981 "Transcultural Use of Narcotic Water Lilies in Ancient Egyptian and Maya Drug Ritual," *Journal of Ethnopharmacology* 2: 173–80.

1982 "The Mushroom and the Water Lily: Literary and Pictorial Evidence for *Nymphaea* as a Ritual Psychotogen in Mesoamerica," *Journal of Ethnopharmacology* 3: 39–83.

EMBODEN, WILLIAM A., AND MARLENE DOBKIN DE RIOS

1981 "Narcotic Ritual Use of Water Lilies Among Ancient Egypt and the Maya," in *Folk Healing and Herbal Medicine*, ed. G. Meyer and K. Blum (Springfield, Ill.: Charles Thomas Publishers).

ENGEL, F.

1966 *Paracas, Cien Siglos de Cultura Perúana* (Lima: Mejia Baca).

ERSPAMER, V. T., ET AL.
1967   "5 Methoxy- and 5-Hydroxyindoles in the Skin of *Bufo Alvarius*," *Biochemical Pharmacology* 14: 1149–64.

EVARTS, E. V.
1956   "Some Effects of Bufotenine and LSD on the Monkey," *AMA Archives of Neurology and Psychiatry* 75: 49–53.

FABING, H. D.
1957   "Toads, Mushrooms, and Schizophrenia," *Harper's* 214: 1284–90.

FABING, H. D., AND J. HAWKINS
1956   "Intravenous Injections of Bufotenine in Man," *Science* 123: 886.

FAIRHOLT, F. W.
1859   *Tobacco, Its History and Associations* (London).

FENTON, WILLIAM N.
1940   "Masked Medicine Societies of the Iroquois," *Smithsonian Institution Annual Report to the Board of Regents* 95: 397–429.

FERNANDEZ, JAMES W.
1965   "Symbolic Consensus in a Fang Reformative Cult," *American Anthropologist* 67: 902–29.

1972   "*Tabernanthe iboga*: Narcotic Ecstasis and the Work of the Ancestors," in *Flesh of the Gods: The Ritual Use of Hallucinogens*, ed. P. T. Furst (New York: Praeger).

1982   *Bwiti: An Ethnography of the Religious Imagination in Africa* (Princeton: Princeton University Press).

FRIEDBERG, CLAUDINE
1960   "Utilisation d'un Cactus à Mescaline au Nord de Perou (*Trichocereus pachanoi*)," *Proceedings of the Sixth International Congress of Anthropological and Ethnological Sciences* 2: 21–26.

1965   "Rapport sur une mission au Perou: description du materiel recuelli, Exposé sommaire des recherches entreprises," *Travaux de l'Institut Français d'Etudes Andines* 7: 65–94.

FURST, PETER J.
1965   "West Mexican Tomb Sculpture as Evidence for Shamanism in Prehistoric Meso-America," *Anthropologica* 15: 29–60.

1968   "The Olmec Were-Jaguar Motif in the Light of Ethnographic Reality," in *Dumbarton Oaks Conference on the Olmec*, ed. Elizabeth P. Benson (Washington, D.C.: Dumbarton Oaks Research Library).

1972   "Symbolism and Psychopharmacology: The Toad as Earth Mother in Indian America," *Sociedad Mexicana de Antropología 13 Mesa Redonda en Mesoamérica* (Mexico City).

ISBELL, H.
1967   "Effects of $(-)\Delta$ 9-Trans-Tetrahydrocannabinol in Man," *Psychopharmacologia* 11: 184–88.

ISBELL, WILLIAM H.
1978   "The Prehistoric Ground Drawings of Peru," *Scientific American* 239: 140–53.

JANIGER, OSCAR, AND MARLENE DOBKIN DE RIOS
1973   "Suggestive Hallucinogenic Properties of Tobacco," *Medical Anthropology Newsletter* 4(4): 6–11.
1976   "Nicotiana an Hallucinogen?" *Economic Botany* 30: 149–51.

JOCELSON, W.
1905   "The Koryak: Part I. Religion and Myth," *Memoirs of the American Museum of Natural History* 6: 148–205.

JOHNSTON, THOMAS F.
1972   "Datura Use in a Tsonga Girls' Puberty School," *Economic Botany* 26(4): 340–51.

JOHNSTON, T. H., AND J. B. CLELLAND
1933   "The History of the Aborigine Narcotic, Pituri," *Oceania* 4(2): 201–23, 268, 289.

JONES, IVOR H.
1969   "Subincision Among Australian Western Desert Aborigines," *British Journal of Medical Psychology* 42: 182–90.

JONES, IVOR H., AND DAVID J. HORNE
1972   "Diagnosis of Psychiatric Illness Among Tribal Aborigines," *Medical Journal of Australia* 1: 345–49.

KARSTEN, RAFAEL
1923   *Blood Revenge, War, and Victory Feasts Among the Jibaro Indians of E. Ecuador,* Bulletin of the Smithsonian Institution no. 79 (Washington, D.C.).
1935   *Headhunters of the Western Amazonas: Life and Culture of Jibaro Indians of Eastern Ecuador and Peru* (Helsinki: Societas Scientarum Fennica).

KATZ, FRED, AND MARLENE DOBKIN DE RIOS
1971   "Hallucinogenic Music: An Analysis of the Role of Whistling in Peruvian Ayahuasca Healing Sessions," *Journal of American Folklore* 84(333): 320–27.

KAUFFMANN, FEDERICO
1976   *El Perú Arqueológico* (Lima: Ediciones Kompaktos).
1978   *Sexual Behavior in Ancient Peru* (Lima: Ediciones Erigraf).

KELLERT, STEPHEN, ET AL.

1967   "Culture Change and Stress in Rural Peru: A Preliminary Report," *Milbank Memorial Fund Quarterly* 45: 4.

KENNEDY, ALISON BAILEY

1982   "Ecco Bufo: The Toad in Nature and Olmec Iconography," *Current Anthropology* 23: 273–90.

KENSINGER, K.

1972   *"Banisteriopsis* and the Cashinahua," in *Hallucinogens and Shamanism,* ed. M. J. Harner (New York: Oxford University Press).

KIRSCHOFF, PAUL

1949   "Tribes North of the Orinoco River," in *Handbook of South American Indians,* ed. J. Steward, vol. 4 (Washington, D.C.: Smithsonian Institution).

KLEINMAN, ARTHUR, AND LILIAS H. SUNG

1979   "Why Do Indigenous Practitioners Successfully Heal?" *Social Science and Medicine* 13B: 7–26.

KLUCKHOHN, CLYDE

1942   "Myths and Rituals: A General Theory," *Harvard Theological Review* 35: 1.

KLUVER, H.

1942   "Mechanisms of Hallucinations," in *Studies in Personality,* ed. Q. McNemar and M. A. Merrill (New York: McGraw-Hill).

KOCH-GRUNBERG, T.

1908   "Die Hianokoto: Umaua," *Antropos* 3: 83, 124, 297–33, 924–28.

KOSKOWSKI, WILLIAM

1957   "The Habit of Tobacco Smoking" in *History of Tobacco,* ed. George Arents, Jr. (London).

KOSOK, PAUL

1947   "The Mysterious Markings of Nazca," *Natural History* 56: 200–209.

KOSOK, PAUL, AND AMARIA REICHE

1949   "Ancient Drawings on the Desert of Peru," *Archaeology* 11: 206–15.

KRIPPNER, S., AND D. FERSH

1971   "Psychic Happenings in Hippy Communes," *Psychic Magazine* 3(3): 40–45.

KUBLER, GEORGE

1962   *The Art and Architecture of Ancient America* (New York: Penguin).

1969   *Studies in Classic Maya Iconography* (Greenwich, Conn.: New York Graphic Society).

KUSEL, H.

1965 "Ayahuasca Drinkers Among the Chama Indians," *Psychedelic Review* 6: 58–63.

KUTSCHER, C.

1950 *Chimu: Eine Altindianische Hochkulture* (Mann).

1967 "Iconographic Studies as an Aid in the Reconstruction of Early Chimu Civilization," in *Peruvian Archaeology: Selected Readings*, ed. J. H. Rowe and D. Menzel (Palo Alto, Calif.: Peek Publications).

LA BARRE, WESTON

1964 *The Peyote Cult* (New York: Schocken Books).

1970a *The Ghost Dance: Origins of Religion* (New York: Random House).

1970b "Old and New World Narcotics: A Statistical Question and an Ethnological Reply," *Economic Botany* 24: 73–80.

1972 "Hallucinogens and the Shamanic Origins of Religion," in *Flesh of the Gods: The Ritual Use of Hallucinogens*, ed. P. T. Furst (New York: Praeger).

LAMB, BRUCE, AND MANUEL CORDOVA-RIOS

1971 *Wizard of the Upper Amazon* (New York: Athenaeum).

LANDA, D. DE

1941 *Relación de las Cosas de Yucatán*, trans. A. M. Tozzer, Papers of the Peabody Museum of Archaeology and Ethnology, vol. 18 (Cambridge, Mass.: Harvard University).

LANNING, E.

1967 *Peru Before the Incas* (Englewood Cliffs, N.J.: Prentice Hall).

LARCO HOYLE, R.

1939 *Los Mochicas*, 2 vols. (Lima).

1969 *Checcan* (New York: Nagel Press).

LASKI, VERA

1958 *Seeking Life* (Philadelphia: American Folklore Society).

LAVALLÉE, D.

1970 *Les Representations Animales dans la Céramique Mochica*, Memoires de l'Institut d'Ethnologie 4 (Paris: Musée de l'Homme).

LEHMAN, W.

1924 *Kunstgeschichte des Alten Peru* (Berlin: Verlag Ernst Wasmuth).

LEMLIJ, M.

1965 "Del Uso de Psicodislépticos en la Selva Perúana," *Perú, Sanidad del Gobierno y Policía*, pp. 195–207.

LEVIN, M. G., AND L. P. POTAPOW, EDS.

1956 *The Peoples of Siberia*, trans. Stephen Dunn (Chicago: University of Chicago Press).

LÉVI-STRAUSS, C.

1963   "The Effectiveness of Symbols," in *Structural Anthropology*, trans.
        C. Jacobson and B. Schoepf (New York: Basic Books).

1970   "Les Champignons dans la Culture: A Propos d'un Livre de
        M. R. G. Wasson," *L'Homme* 10(1): 5–16.

LEWIN, L.

1928   "Untersuchungen uber Banisteria Caapi Spr.," *Archiv. fur Ex-
        periment Path. u Pharmakol.* 219: 133–49.

1964   *Phantastica: Narcotic and Stimulating Drugs, Their Use and Abuse*
        (New York: E. P. Dutton).

LI, HUI-LIN

1975   "The Origin and Use of Cannabis in Eastern Asia: Their Lin-
        guistic-Cultural Implications," in *Cannabis and Culture*, ed.
        V. Rubin (The Hague: Mouton Press).

LOMAX, A.

1968   *Folk Songs, Style and Culture* (Washington, D.C.: American As-
        sociation for the Advancement of Science).

LOWE, G. W., AND J. A. MASON

1965   "Archaeological Survey of the Chiapas Coast, Highlands, and
        Upper Grijalva Basin," in *Handbook of Middle American Indians*,
        vol. 2, *Archaeology of Southern Mesoamerica*, ed. R. Wauchope
        and G. R. Willey (Austin: University of Texas Press).

LOWIE, ROBERT H.

1954   *Indians of the Plains* (New York: American Museum Science Books).

LOWY, B.

1971   "New Records of Mushroom Stones from Guatemala," *Myco-
        logia* 63: 983–93.

LUDWIG, ARNOLD

1969   "Altered States of Consciousness," in *Altered States of Conscious-
        ness*, ed. Charles Tart (New York: Wiley).

McALLESTER, DAVID P.

1949   *Peyote Music*, Viking Fund Publication in Anthropology no. 13
        (New York; reprint ed.: Johnson Reprints).

McGUIRE, JOSEPH

1898   *Pipes and Smoking Customs of the American Aborigines, Based on
        Materials from the U.S. National Museum* (Washington, D.C.:
        Smithsonian Institution).

McGUIRE, THOMAS M.

1982   "Ancient Maya Mushroom Connection: A Transcendental
        Interaction Model," *Journal of Psychoactive Drugs* 14(3): 221–
        38.

MACKENZIE, D. A.
1924 *Myths of Pre-Columbian America* (London).
MARSHALL, C. R.
1937 "An Enquiry into the Causes of Mescal Vision," *Journal of Neuropathy and Psychopathology* 17: 289–304.
MARTIN, R. T.
1970 "The Role of Coca," *Economic Botany* 24: 422–38.
MASTERS, R. E. L., AND JEAN HOUSTON
1966 *The Varieties of Psychedelic Experience* (New York: Dell).
MEANS, P. A.
1917 "A Survey of Ancient Peruvian Art," *Transactions of the Connecticut Academy of Arts and Sciences* 21: 315–442.
MEJIA, T.
1949 "Acueductores y Caminos," *Proceedings of the Twenty-ninth International Congress of Americanists* (Chicago: University of Chicago Press).
METRAUX, ALFRED
1949 "The Tucuna," in *Handbook of South American Indians,* ed. J. Steward, vol. 5 (Washington, D.C.: Smithsonian Institution).
MEYERHOFF, BARBARA
1975 "Organization and Ecstasy: Deliberate and Accidental Communities among Huichol and American Youth," in *Symbols and Politics in Communal Ideology,* ed. Sally Falk Moore and Barbara G. Meyerhoff (Ithaca: Cornell University Press).
MILES, S. W.
1965 "Sculpture of the Guatemalan-Chiapas Highlands and Pacific Slopes and Associated Hieroglyphs," in *Archaeology of Southern Mesoamerica, Handbook of Middle American Indians,* vol. 2, ed. R. Wauchope and G. R. Willey (Austin: University of Texas Press).
MILLER, WALTER
1966 "El Tonalamatl Mixe y los Hongos Sagrados," in *Summa Antropológica en Homenaje a Roberto J. Weitlaner* (Mexico City: Instituto Nacional de Antropología e Historia).
MORLEY, S. G.
1956 *The Ancient Maya,* ed. G. Brainerd (Stanford: Stanford University Press).
MORTIMER, W. G.
1901 *Peru, History of Coca, the Divine Plant* (New York: Vail).
MUELLE, J. C.
1937 "Filogenia de la Estela de Raimondi," *Revista del Museo Nacional, Lima* 4.

MUNDKUR, BALAJI
1976   "The Cult of the Serpent in the Americas: Its Asian Background," *Current Anthropology* 17(3): 429–57.
MUNN, H.
1973   "The Mushrooms of Language," in *Hallucinogens and Shamanism*, ed. Michael J. Harner (New York: Oxford University Press).
MURPHREE, HENRY B.
1967   "The Effects of Nicotine and Smoking on the Central Nervous System," *Annals of the New York Academy of Sciences* 142: 1–133.
NARANJO, CLAUDIO
1967   "Psychotropic Properties of the Harmala Alkaloids," in *Ethnopharmacologic Search for Psychoactive Drugs*, ed. Daniel Efron (Washington, D.C.: U.S. Government Printing Office).
NARANJO, P.
1969   "Etnofarmacología de las Plantas Psicotrópicas de América," *Terápia* 24(1): 5–63 (Quito, Ecuador).
NEHER, ANDREW
1962   "A Physiological Explanation of Unusual Behavior in Ceremonies Involving Drums," *Human Biology* 34: 151–60.
NELSON, H.
1970   "On the Etiology of Mushroom Madness in Highland New Guinea: Kaimbi Culture and Psychrotropism," paper presented at the Sixty-ninth Annual Meeting of the American Anthropological Association, San Diego.
ORTIZ DE MONTELLANO, B.
1975   "Empirical Aztec Medicine," *Science* 188(4185): 215–20.
OVIEDO, JESUS
1964   *Estudio Socio-Económico de la Barriada "El Puerto de Belén" de la Ciudad de Iquitos* (Lima: Escuela de Servicio Social).
PAHNKE, W. N.
1967   "The Contribution of the Psychology of Religion to the Therapeutic Use of Psychedelic Substances," in *The Use of LSD in Psychotherapy and Alcoholism*, ed. Harold A. Abramson (New York: Bobbs-Merrill).
PENNES, HARRY H., AND PAUL HOCH
1957   "Psychotomimetics, Clinical and Theoretical Considerations: Harmine, Win-2299 and Nalline," *American Journal of Psychiatry* 113: 887–92.
PEREZ DE BARRADAS, J.
1950   "Drogas Ilusionógenas de los Indios Americanos," *Antropología y Etnología* 3: 9–107.

PETERS, L., AND D. R. PRICE-WILLIAMS
1980   "Toward an Experiential Analysis of Shamanism," *American Ethnologist* 7: 397–418.

PEZZIA, A.
1972   *Arqueología del Departamento de Ica* (Ica, Peru).

PITT-RIVERS, J.
1970   "Spiritual Power in Central America: The Naguals of Chiapas," in *Witchcraft Confessions and Accusations,* ed. Mary Douglas (New York: Tavistock).

PLOWMAN, T.
1981   "Amazonian Coca," *Journal of Ethnopharmacology* 3: 195–225.

POINDEXTER, E. H., AND R. D. CARPENTER
1962a   "Isolation of Harman and Norharman from Cigarette Smoke," *Chemistry and Industry* 27:176.
1962b   "Isolation of Harman and Norharman from Tobacco and Cigarette Smoke," *Phytochemistry* 1: 215–21 (London: Pergamon).

POKORNY, A.
1970   "The Hallucinogens in Anthropology, Pre-history, and the History of the Plastic Arts," paper read at the Seventh Congress of the Collegium Internationale, Neuro-Psychopharma-Cologium, Prague.

POPE, H. G.
1969   "Tabernanthe iboga: An African Narcotic Plant of Social Importance," *Economic Botany* 23(2): 174–84.

PRANCE, G.
1970   "Notes on the Use of Plant Hallucinogens in Amazonian Brazil," *Economic Botany* 24: 1–17.

PROSKOURIAKOFF, T.
1965   "Sculpture and Major Art of the Lowland Maya," in *Handbook of Middle American Indians,* vol. 2, *Archaeology of Southern Mesoamerica,* ed. R. Wauchope and G. R. Willey (Austin: University of Texas Press).

PROULX, D.
1968   *Local Differences and Time Differences in Nazca Pottery,* University of California Publications in Anthropology 5 (Berkeley).

RANDS, R. L.
1953   "The Water Lily in Maya Art: A Complex of Alleged Asiatic Origin," *Bureau of American Ethnology Bulletin* 151: 73–153 (Washington, D.C.: Smithsonian Institution).
1955   "Some Manifestations of Water in Mesoamerican Art," *Bureau*

of *American Ethnology Bulletin* 157: 265–393 (Washington, D.C.: Smithsonian Institution).

RAPPAPORT, ROY

1971   "Ritual, Sanctity and Cybernetics," *American Anthropologist* 73(1): 59–76.

RAVICZ, ROBERT

1960   "La Mixteca en el Estudio Comparativo del Hongo Alucinante," *Anales del Instituto Nacional de Antropología e História* 13: 73–92.

REAY, M.

1959   *The Kuma: Freedom and Conformity in the New Guinea Highlands* (Melbourne: Australian National University Press).

1960   "Mushroom Madness in the New Guinea Highlands," *Oceania* 31(3): 137–39.

REICHE, MARIA

1949   *Los Dibujos Gigantescos en el Suelo de las Pampas de Nasca y Palpa* (Lima).

1978   *Mystery on the Desert* (Lima: Editorial Médica Perúana).

REICHEL-DOLMATOFF, GERALDO

1971   *Amazonian Cosmos: The Sexual and Religious Symbolism of the Tukano Indians* (Chicago: University of Chicago Press).

1972   "The Cultural Context of an Aboriginal Hallucinogen, *Banisteriopsis caapi*," in *Flesh of the Gods: The Ritual Use of Hallucinogens*, ed. P. T. Furst (New York: Praeger).

REINA, RUBEN

1969   "Eastern Guatemalan Highlands: The Pokomames and Chorti," in *Handbook of Middle American Indians*, vol. 7, pt. 1, ed. R. Wauchope (Austin: University of Texas Press).

REINBURG, P.

1965   *Bebidas Tóxicas de los Indios del Amazonas: El Ayahuasca–El Yaje–El Huanto*, Universidad Nacional Mayor de San Marcos Ciencia Nueva, vol. 4 (Lima).

RIBIERO, DARCY

1971   *The Americas and Civilization*, trans. L. Barrett (New York: E. P. Dutton).

RIVIERE, L., AND J. E. LINDGREN

1972   "Ayahuasca, the South American Hallucinogenic Drink: An Ethnobotanical and Chemcial Investigation," *Economic Botany* 26: 2–17.

ROARK, P. R.

1965   "From Monumental to Proliferous in Nazca Pottery," *Nawpa Pacha* 3: 1–92.

ROBERTSON, MERLE GREENE
1972 "The Ritual Bundles of Yaxchilan," paper presented at the Tulane University Symposium on the Art of Latin America, New Orleans.

ROBICSEK, FRANCIS
1978 *The Smoking Gods: Tobacco in Maya Art, History and Religion* (Norman: University of Oklahoma Press).

ROESSNER, TOMAS
1946 "El Ayahuasca, Planta Mágica del Amazonas," *Revista Geográfica Americana* 29: 14–16 (Buenos Aires).

ROTH, WALTER E.
1897 *Ethnological Studies among the Northwest Central Queensland Aborigines* (London: E. Gregory).
1915 *An Inquiry into the Animism and Folklore of the Guina Indians,* Thirtieth Annual Report of the Bureau of American Ethnology (Washington, D.C.: Smithsonian Institution).

ROWE, J. H.
1960 "Nuevos Datos Relativos a la Cronología del Estilo Nasca," in *Antíguo Peru, Espacio y Tiempo* (Lima: Editorial Mejia Baca).
1961 "La Arqueología de Ica," *Revista del Museo Regional de Ica* 12: 29–48.

ROYS, R. L.
1931 *The Ethnobotany of the Maya,* Tulane University Publication no. 2 (New Orleans: Middle American Research Institute; reprint Philadelphia: ISHI, 1976).

RUBEL, ARTHUR J., AND JEAN GETTELFINGER-KREJCI
n.d. "The Use of Hallucinogenic Mushrooms for Diagnostic Purposes Among Some Highland Chinantecs" (manuscript, Dept. of Family Medicine, University of California, Irvine).

RUBIN, VERA
1976 *Cannabis and Culture* (The Hague: Mouton Press).

RYDEN, S.
1930 "Une Tête Trophée de Nasca," *Journal de la Société des Americanistes* (Paris).

SAFFORD, W. E.
1916 "Narcotic Plants and Stimulants of the Ancient Americas," *Annual Report* (Washington, D.C.: Smithsonian Institution).

SALER, BENSON
1964 "Nagual, Witch and Sorcerer in a Quiche Village," *Ethnology* 3: 305–28.

SAL Y ROSAS, FEDERICO

1958   "El Mito de Jani o Susto de la Medicina Indígena del Perú,"
        Revista de la Sanidad de Policia 18: 167–210.

SATTERTHWAITE, LINTON

1943   Notes on the Sculpture and Architecture at Tonala, Chiapas, Carnegie
        Institution of Washington Notes on Middle American Archae-
        ology and Ethnology, vol. 1, nos. 1–30 (Washington, D.C.).

SAWYER, A. R.

1966   Ancient Peruvian Ceramics: The Nathan Cummings Collection, Met-
        ropolitan Museum of Art (Greenwich, Conn.: New York Graphic
        Society).

SCHLESIER, K. H.

1959   "Stilgeschichtliche Einordung der Nazca Vasenmalereien: Bei-
        tray zur Geschicht der Hochkulturen des Vorkolumbischen Peru,"
        Annali Lateranensi 23: 9–236.

SCHULTES, RICHARD EVANS

1941   A Contribution to our Knowledge of Rivea Corymbosa: The Narcotic
        Ololiuqui of the Aztecs (Cambridge, Mass.: Botanical Museum of
        Harvard).

1957   "The Identity of Malpighiaceous Narcotics of South America,"
        Harvard University Botanical Museum Leaflets 18: 1 (June).

1960   Native Narcotics of the New World, The Pharmacologic Sciences,
        Third Lecture Series (London).

1967   "The Place of Ethnobotany in the Ethnopharmacologic Search
        for Psychoto-Mimetic Drugs," in Ethnopharmacologic Search for
        Psychoactive Drugs, ed. D. Efron (Washington, D.C.: U.S. Gov-
        ernment Printing Office).

1970   "The Botanical and Chemical Distribution of Hallucinogens,"
        Annual Review of Plant Physiology 21: 571–98.

1972a   "An Overview of Hallucinogens in the Western Hemisphere,"
        in Flesh of the Gods: The Ritual Use of Hallucinogens, ed. P. T. Furst
        (New York: Praeger).

1972b   "The Ethnotoxicological Significance of Additives to New World
        Hallucinogens," Plant Science Bulletin 18: 34–40.

SCHULTES, RICHARD EVANS, AND ALBERT HOFMANN

1973   The Botany and Chemistry of Hallucinogens (Springfield, Ill.: Charles
        C. Thomas Publishers).

SELER, E.

1923   "Die Buntbemalten Gefasse von Nasca im Sudlichen Peru und
        die Hauptlemente Ihrer Verzierung," Gesemmelte Abhandlungen
        zur Amerikanischen Sprach- und Alterhumskunde von Edeward Seler,

Herausgegeben von Caecilie Seler-Sachs (Berlin: Vierter Band Behrend).

SHARER, ROBERT

1968 "Pre-Classic Archaeological Investigations at Chalchuapa, El Salvador: The El Trapiche Mound Group (Ph.D. diss., University of Pennsylvania).

SHARON, DOUGLAS

1972a "Eduardo the Healer," *Natural History* 81: 32–47.

1972b "The San Pedro Cactus in Peruvian Folk Healing," in *Flesh of the Gods: The Ritual Use of Hallucinogens*, ed. P. T. Furst (New York: Praeger).

SHARON, DOUGLAS, AND C. B. DONNAN

1974 "Shamanism in Moche Iconography," in *Ethnoarchaeology*, ed. C. Donnan and C. W. Clewlow, Jr., University of California Institute of Archaeology Monograph 4 (Los Angeles).

SHELLHAS, PAUL

1904 *Representations of Deities of the Maya Manuscripts*, Papers of the Peabody Museum of American Archaeology and Ethnology, vol. 4, no. 1 (Cambridge, Mass.: Harvard University).

SHOOK, E. M., AND A. V. KIDDER

1952 *Mound E-III-3, Kaminaljuyu, Guatemala*, Carnegie Institution of Washington Contributions to American Anthropology and History 53, Publication 596 (Washington, D.C.).

SIEGEL, RONALD K.

1973 "An Ethnological Search for Self-Administration of Hallucinogens," *International Journal of the Addictions* 8: 373–93.

SISKIND, J.

1973 "Visions and Cures Among the Sharanahua," in *Hallucinogens and Shamanism*, ed. M. J. Harner (New York: Oxford University Press).

SKINNER, ALANSON

1915 *Societies of the Ioway, Kansa, and Ponce Indians*, Anthropological Papers of the American Museum of Natural History 11 (New York).

SMITH, DAVID E.

1970 "LSD, Radical Religious Beliefs," *Journal of Psychedelic Drugs* 3(1): 38–41.

1977 "Adverse Drug Reactions from a Rock Medical Team Report," *Journal of the Addiction Research Foundation*, February 1 (Toronto).

SOLLMANN, TORALD

1947 *A Manual of Pharmacology*, 7th ed. (Philadelphia: W. B. Saunders).

SPENCER, B., AND F. J. GILLEN
1899   *Native Tribes of Central Australia* (London: Macmillan & Co.).

SPENCER, ROBERT F., ET AL.
1965   *The Native Americans* (New York: Harper & Row, Publishers).

SPINDLER, G. D.
1955   "Sociocultural and Psychological Processes in Menomini Acculturation," *University of California Publications in Culture and Society* 5: 430–53.

SPRUCE, RICHARD
1908   *Notes of a Botanist on the Amazon and Andes*, vol. 2 (London: Macmillan & Co.).

STAFFORD, P.
1977   *Psychedelic Encyclopedia* (Berkeley, Calif.: And/Or Press).

STAT, DANIEL K.
1974   "Double-Chambered Whistling Bottles: A Unique Peruvian Pottery Form," *Journal of Transpersonal Psychology* 6(2): 157–62.

STEWARD, JULIAN
1949   "The Circum-Caribbean Tribes," in *Handbook of South American Indians*, ed. J. Steward, vol. 4 (Washington, D.C.: Smithsonian Institution).

STEWARD, JULIAN, AND LOUIS C. FARON
1959   *Native Peoples of South America* (New York: McGraw-Hill).

STOWE, B. B.
1959   "Occurrence and Metabolism of Simple Indoles in Plants," in *Fortschrift der Chemie Organischer Naturstoffe*, ed. L. Zechmeister (Vienna).

SWIDERSKI, S.
1965   "Le Bwiti: Société d'initiation chez les Apindji au Gabon," *Antropos* 60: 541–51.

TART, CHARLES
1971   *On Being Stoned: A Psychological Study of Marihuana Intoxication* (Palo Alto, Calif.: Science and Behavior Books).

1972a   *Altered States of Consciousness* (New York: John Wiley & Sons).

1972b   "States of Consciousness and State-Specific Sciences," *Science* 176: 1203–10.

1975   *Transpersonal Psychologies* (New York: Harper and Row, Publishers).

TAYLOR, J. C.
1977   "A Pre-Contact Aboriginal Medical System on Cape York Peninsula," *Journal of Human Evolution* 6: 419–32.

TAYLOR, NORMAN
1966   *Narcotics: Nature's Dangerous Gifts* (New York: Dell).
TELLO, JULIO C.
1915   "Los Antiguos Cementerios del Valle de Nasca," *Second Congress of Panamerican Sciences* (Washington, D.C.).
TESTA, A., AND P. TESTA
1965   "Nitrogenous Heterocyclic Compounds in (Cigarette) Smoke Condensates," *Directoire Annual des Etudes Equipements SEITA* 2 (section 1), pp. 163–91.
THOMPSON, J. ERIC S.
1950   *Maya Hieroglyphic Writing*, Carnegie Institute of Washington, Publication 589 (Washington, D.C.).
1954   *The Rise and Fall of Maya Civilization* (Norman: University of Oklahoma Press).
1965   "Archaeological Synthesis of the Southern Maya Lowlands," in *Archaeological of Southern Mesoamerica, Handbook of Middle American Indians*, vol. 2, ed. R. Wauchope and G. R. Willey (Austin: University of Texas Press).
1970   *Maya History and Religion* (Norman: University of Oklahoma Press).
TORO, ALFONSO
1954   "Las Plantas Sagradas de los Aztecas y su Influencia sobre el Arte Precortesiano," *Proceedings of the Twenty-third International Congress of Americanists.*
TOWLE, M.
1961   *The Ethnobotany of Pre-Columbian Peru*, Viking Fund Publication in Anthropology no. 30 (New York).
        (New York)
TOZZER, ALFRED, AND G. ALLEN
1910   *Animal Figures in the Maya Codices*, Papers of the Peabody Museum of Archaeology and Ethnology 4, no. 3 (Cambridge, Mass.: Harvard University).
TURNER, VICTOR
1974   *Dramas, Fields, and Metaphors: Symbolic Action in Human Society* (Ithaca: Cornell University Press).
UHLE, MAX
1914   "The Nasca Pottery of Ancient Peru," *Davenport Academy of Sciences Proceedings* (Davenport, Conn.).
URTEAGA-BALLON, O.
1968   *Interpretacíon de la Sexualidad en la Cerámica del Antiguo Perú* (Lima: Health Sciences Museum).

244 REFERENCES

VALDIVIA, OSCAR
1964 *Historia de la Psiquiatría Perúana* (Lima: Universidad Nacional Mayor de San Marcos).
VILLAVICENCIO, M.
1858 *Geography of the Republic of Ecuador* (New York: Graighead).
VOGEL, V.
1969 *American Indian Medicine* (Norman, Okla.: University of Oklahoma Press).
VOGT, EVON Z., AND ALBERTO RUZ LHUILLIER, EDS.
1964 *Desarollo Cultural de Los Mayas* (Mexico City: Universidad Nacional Autonoma de Mexico).
VON WINNING, HASSO
1969 "A Toad Effigy Vessel from Nayarit," *The Masterkey* 43: 29–32.
WAGLEY, CHARLES
1943 "Tapirape Shamanism," *Museu Nacional Boletin* 3: 41–94 (Rio de Janeiro).
WALLACE, ANTHONY F. C.
1959 "Cultural Determinants of Response to Hallucinatory Experience," *AMA Archives of General Psychiatry* 1: 58–69.
1966 *Religion: An Anthropological View* (New York: Random House).
1971 "A Possible Technique for Recognizing Psychological Characteristics of the Ancient Maya from an Analysis of Their Art," in *Art and Aesthetics in Primitive Societies*, ed. Carol F. Jopling (New York: E. P. Dutton).
WASSEN, S. H.
1934 "The Frog-Motif Among the South American Indians," *Antropos* 29: 319–70; part II: "The Frog in Indian Mythology and Imagination World," *Antropos* 29: 613–58.
WASSON, R. GORDON
1966 "Ololiuqui and Other Hallucinogens of Mexico," in *Summa Antropológica en Homenaje a Roberto J. Weitlander* (Mexico: Instituto Nacional de Antropología e Historia).
1967 "Fly Agaric and Man," in *The Ethnopharmacologic Search for Psychoactive Drugs*, ed. D. Efron (Washington, D.C.: U.S. Government Printing Office).
1968 *Soma, Divine Mushroom of Immortality* (New York: Harcourt, Brace & World).
1972 "What Was the Soma of the Aryans?" in *Flesh of the Gods: The Ritual Use of Hallucinogens*, ed. P. T. Furst (New York: Praeger).
WASSON, R. G., AND V. P. WASSON
1957 *Russia, Mushrooms and History*, 2 vols. (New York: Pantheon).

WEBB, CLARENCE H.
1971   "Archaic and Poverty Point Zoomorphic Locust Beads," *American Antiquity* 36: 105–14.

WIFFEN, THOMAS
1915   *The Northwest Amazonas: Notes of Some Months Spent Among Cannibal Tribes* (London: Constable).

WHITMAN, WILLIAM
1940   "The San Ildefonso of New Mexico," in *Acculturation in Seven American Indian Tribes*, ed. Ralph Linton (New York: Appleton-Century-Crofts).

WILBERT, JOHANNES
1972   "Tobacco and Shamanistic Ecstasy among the Warao Indians of Venezuela," in *Flesh of the Gods: The Ritual Use of Hallucinogens*, ed. P. T. Furst (New York: Praeger).

WILS, FRITS
1966   *Estudio Social Sobre Belen—Iquitos* (Lima: Centro de Investigaciones Sociales, Economicas, Politicas y Anthropologicas).

YACOVLEFF, E. N.
1932   "La Deidad Primitiva de los Nasca," *Revista del Museo Nacional* 1: 101–60 (Lima).
1934   "El Mundo Vegetal de los Antiguos Perúanos," *Revista del Museo Nacional* 3: 241–322 (Lima).

ZINBERG, N. E., AND R. C. JACOBSON
1976   "The Natural History of 'Chipping,'" *American Journal of Psychiatry* 133(1): 37–40.

ZINBERG, N. E., R. C. JACOBSON, AND W. M. HARDING
1975   "Social Sanctions and Rituals as a Basis for Drug Abuse Prevention," *American Journal of Drug and Alcohol Abuse* 2(2): 165–82.

ZUIDEMA, R. T.
1971   "Meaning in Nazca Art: Iconographic Relationships Between Inca Huari and Nazca Cultures in Southern Peru," *Goteborgs Etnografiska Museut Aarstryck*, pp. 35–54.

ZUKAV, GARY
1979   *The Dancing Wu Li Masters: An Overview of the New Physics* (New York: William Morrow).

Index